Fruitful Rewarding Years

FRUITFUL REWARDING YEARS
A SUBMARINER'S STORY

by

SAM FRY

The Memoir Club

© Sam Fry 2006

First published in 2006 by
The Memoir Club
Stanhope Old Hall
Stanhope
Weardale
County Durham

British Library Cataloguing in
Publication Data.
A catalogue record for this book
is available from the
British Library

ISBN: 1-84104-150-5

Typeset by TW Typesetting, Plymouth, Devon
Printed by CPI, Bath

Contents

List of Illustrations

Foreword

by
Vice Admiral Sir Lancelot Bell Davies KBE[1]

Sam Fry's naval career spanned a period of history wherein the Royal Navy declined dramatically in size, but accelerated in technological development.

The Sub-Lieutenant Fry I met in 1951 was an enthusiastic trainee submariner. He had an excellent brain and he knew it. He was very determined, very capable, very forthright and very self-confident.

The Commander Fry with whom I served sixteen years later was all of those things, but he had added wisdom and experience to his talents. A well-developed sense of humour and humanity tempered his impatience with imperfections. It was a joy to be working with him.

His remarkably detailed, and fascinating, account of his time in the Service is full of the fun and games of a naval career. The reader is however aware that, behind the levity, lies a tale of outstanding professionalism and dedication to a branch of the Navy wherein any one sailor's error can sink the boat, which makes the training of that sailor rather important.

---

[1] Admiral Bell Davies is the son of the famous Vice Admiral Richard Bell Davies VC CB DSO AFC. He joined Dartmouth as a 13-year-old cadet in 1939 and after service in HMS *Norfolk* joined submarines in 1944. His first Submarine Command was HMS *Subtle*. He was the first CO of HMS *Explorer* before being the 'Teacher' to the Submarine COs' Course. In 1963 he took command of HMS *Leander*, the first ship of class. As a Captain he was the Naval Assistant to the Controller of the Navy. He then commanded the 7th Submarine Squadron and HMS *Forth* in Singapore. After 3 years as Director of Naval Warfare he commanded HMS *Bulwark*, a Commando carrier equipped with helicopters. After promotion to Rear Admiral he was Chief of the British Naval Staff in Washington. Later as SACLANTREPEUR in Brussels he was promoted to Vice Admiral. In 1978 he became Commandant of the NATO Defence College in Rome, and retired in 1981. He was Chairman of the Sea Cadet Council from 1983 to 1991.

Preface by the Author

Luckily for me my naval life was one continuous 'Happy Ship'. I am indebted to Captain Peter Cazalet, who was the Captain of HMS *London* when I was a midshipman, for his definition of a 'Happy Ship', for it really did apply to the lovely *London* in 1949.

He wrote 'If the word "happy" implied just fun and frolic then it is not the word for *London*. But it means much more than this. It means that indefinable force which binds a company of men together, which gives them justifiable pride in their ship and in themselves, and makes them feel that they together can surmount with confidence any emergency which may arise.'

I have been fortunate to command five submarines and a destroyer. I was definitely lucky to have the opportunity to do so. Additionally I was the 'Teacher' to the Submarine Commanding Officers' Qualifying Course for two years and was the first Captain Submarine Sea Training. My last submarine job was a doddle for it was to Command the Polaris Submarine Squadron, an organization that ran on very smooth lines with well oiled wheels and a rigid timetable.

My childhood started with a mother and father who gave me the love and encouragement to do one's best in this life and thus to enter the Royal Navy. So my luck started, and I met my wife by accident and have had over 50 years of happy and supportive marriage so necessary in the modern world as well as a naval career. She has provided us with three lovely children and had the responsibility of successfully raising them whilst I was away for longish periods. That was one of the penalties of naval life.

This account is therefore just one sailor's tale of an enjoyable and formative period in this island's history. It is a story of much change in the Royal Navy, not all for the better by any means, but that is one of the perils of progress however occasioned.

This story is solely my experience. I just hope that it might encourage those who may be interested in a naval career. One

objective is to advertise that branch of the RN which occupied the
major part of my naval years, the Submarine Service. It has been a
great privilege to have been a member and to have enjoyed the
company of so many truly stalwart people.

Sam Fry
Whitchurch Canonicorum
2005

Introduction

I believe Napoleon used to enquire about his generals – 'Is he lucky?' Whilst you can make your own luck, I have been more than reasonably lucky during my life.

My guardian angel directed my path successfully on at least three major occasions. Firstly when I was a cadet in the Training Cruiser. I tried to change from Seaman to Electrical Officer. One of the cadets had done this and the prospect of Cambridge University was very attractive to a 17-year-old, especially as my brother was there. Fortunately my request was refused.

The second lucky break was when I met my wife via a blind date arranged by Hugh Begg who was then a Sub Lieutenant. He had travelled back in HMS *Trump* from Malta to the UK when I was serving in her as the Torpedo Officer. I believe he said that I was not too bad for a 'Dart' (i.e. a Dartmouth entry cadet as opposed to a Special Entry one, which he had been).

The third time was when my angel intervened in 1956. The Royal Navy was then suffering a major axe. Indeed Giles, the *Daily Express* cartoonist, had a picture of the Home Fleet in silhouette showing a cruiser escorted by four destroyers! Many officers were accepting redundancy with what was then termed a 'golden bowler'. I started the ball rolling for a transfer to the Canadian Navy, which would naturally have meant emigrating. The Canadians would not guarantee me service in submarines so I withdrew.

Since then good fortune has shone on many occasions, but never so dramatically as these three interventions.

I have provided a Glossary at the end as I realize that initials and naval parlance can be confusing. Where it is necessary the text includes some explanation of initials before they are used. I have not attempted to go into technical explanations as this is the story of my life, mainly the naval side, and not a text book!

CHAPTER 1

Early days

To 1941

MY EARLIEST MEMORY MUST BE my first flight in an aeroplane, a monoplane in the Isle of Wight when I was four years old. The memory is kept alive by a photograph of me alongside the plane at Newport airport. We used to go to the Isle of Wight for a summer holiday and the beaches at Sandown and Shanklin are well remembered, as are sandcastles, paddleboats and ham sandwiches on the beach. A ham sandwich must have some sand to give it the authentic taste.

We lived in a terraced house in Tennyson Road at Copnor in Portsmouth. My father's parents lived next door. It was later in life that I realized that this arrangement tied my parents to this way of living for many years, much to my mother's chagrin.

My first school was George Street Infants School, which was only a short distance from our house. My form mistress was Miss Young who my mother said used to point to us lads and say that we were her future naval officers. I don't know whether this is true but it does make a good story!

It was not until the war that 'enemy action' caused us to move elsewhere. We had two bombings close by. The first was in a daylight raid when we were just about to sit down to tea. The glass from the window was blown all over the tea table. I was under the table! The second occasion was an unexploded one in virtually the same place as the first and just a matter of yards away from our Anderson shelter at the end of our garden. We then had to move to rented accommodation in Chasewater Avenue, also in Copnor. The effects of bombing still remained with us as St Cuthbert's Church at the end of the road took the full blast of a landmine one night. This explosion blew all our windows out! We then had the steel table-like shelter in the house. I learnt most of my three books of Euclid in the Anderson shelter and slept quite well on one side.

1

I presume that my parents dozed for much of the time seated on the other side. My brother had been evacuated to Winchester.

Portsmouth attracted a certain amount of bombing, as it was an important naval target with its large Dockyard where my father worked. The incendiary raid which destroyed much of the city also demolished my school, which was then Esplanade House School in Southsea. That morning I trudged through lots of debris from Copnor to Southsea, as there were no buses, and found that the school no longer existed as it had been burnt to the ground. Much of Southsea suffered the same fate. So my satchel and all my books were reduced to ashes. Our school later took up residence in a church hall with all ages mixed in together. It seemed to work!

Obviously someone born and bred in Portsmouth would have been interested in the Navy. The Dockyard employed a vast number of people. The ships were a sight to be enjoyed both from Sallyport at the entrance to the harbour and at Navy Days in August. Therefore, at a young age, I saw the great battleships coming into harbour and even walked on their decks during Navy Days.

The fleet review in 1937 for the Coronation was a magnificent sight and I remember travelling between the lines of ships in a paddle steamer. We waved at the *Graf Spee* little realizing that soon she was to be an adversary at the Battle of the River Plate and doomed to an ignominious end.

There was one event in the sea just off Lee on Solent when we witnessed a mock battle between Swordfish aircraft and 'junks'. I do not know the reason for this spectacle but I can still remember it and I must have been very young. Portsmouth was a lively place then. There were three theatres where plays were shown and music hall turns could be seen. There were a vast number of cinemas, and as there was no television and only the radio or reading for leisure time the films figured very much as a way of life. This gave me an everlasting thirst for seeing as many as I could. The law prevented unaccompanied children going to any film classified above 'U'. I used to stand wistfully outside cinemas and ask people to take me in with them. It worked well, particularly with old ladies who often paid for my ticket and took me to the expensive seats. I even managed this method of entry for 'H' for horror films when children had to be over 14 and I was not yet 10! The only 'A' film that I failed to see this way was *Stagecoach*, and I had to return home without seeing it.

I suppose I became obsessive about Chemistry when I was 11 years old onwards. Having an elder brother helped! At that age most boys had a go at making gunpowder and attempts at rocketry. Nowadays they don't appear to know how to strike a match and children are so protected that they are denied the thirst for experiment. Without the benefits of overprotectiveness I did manage to fill the kitchen with chlorine gas, as the rubber cork on my retort leaked. It is true that chlorine is a green gas! I had two near misses with my thirst for knowledge. I made nitrogen tri-iodide by dissolving iodine crystals in nitric acid. I filtered the result onto a filter paper and let it dry out overnight, planning to bottle it next day. That night I read a bit further and found out that nitrogen tri-iodide was a very unstable explosive substance. Next day I picked up the filter paper with my crucible tongs and let it float gently to the floor of the shed where I worked. It exploded with a deafening bang on reaching the ground. The next more catastrophic event involved my attempt to ignite a hydrogen flame from my flask of sulphuric acid and zinc. It should have generated a nice rich gas but unfortunately for me there was air present when I lit the hydrogen. There was a big bang. The thistle funnel shot out of the flask, which exploded quite near to my face. The only injury I sustained was a cut finger. If I had not joined the Navy I would have taken up a career in Chemistry!

Autumn 1941 to 1943: evacuation to Winchester

I was evacuated to Winchester in the autumn of 1941 to join my new school, where I was taken in by Mr and Mrs Saltmarsh who lived in Owens Road opposite the entrance to Peter Symonds School. He was a chauffeur and odd job man to a fairly wealthy lady who lived locally. He had fought in Mesopotamia in the First World War against 'Johnny Turk'. My school shared the premises of Winton House School and Peter Symonds depending upon the days of the week. My brother had been evacuated much earlier in the war and he was well ensconced in Winchester. Initially he had been billeted with Mr and Mrs Turner. Mr Turner was a railway signalman. Later on he moved to the Misses Hilliard. I suppose they shared out the billets then so as to give equal pain to the people of Winchester! Sunday tea was to become a welcome event as I was invited to take tea with the Misses Hilliard, where we had several different kinds of cake!

Life was to be very enjoyable away from Portsmouth and home! It was a carefree existence with lots of chums, plenty of places to explore, the joys of stamp collecting and playing with my expanding collection of lead soldiers and army equipment. Winchester was small compared to Portsmouth and I used to refer to it as 'The Dump', rather unkindly in retrospect. I do remember we walked everywhere in the war years and really covered quite long distances.

Both the Great Western and Southern Railways went through Winchester so it was an excellent place for trainspotting. I gained a lifelong love for railways, although it was to be many years before I gained my very own electric railway. People who have never seen the great steam locomotives that travelled the tracks then have missed out on seeing some marvellous sights.

We found plenty to do in the outdoors. Many hours were spent at the Lido, an outdoor swimming pool, with plenty of space and depth. There were no lifeguards then! We spent a lot of time playing cricket, including bowling at a single stump each end to test for accuracy. My classmates were a splendid group of characters and I can never remember any fighting or bullying. I wonder what has changed these days.

I always enjoyed schoolwork as it came easily to me. We did Latin and French, which were fun. Stamp collecting became a major interest and we made frequent visits to an engraver's shop behind Woolworth's. He used to sell and buy stamps as a sideline and was very kind to us young lads who did not have much money to spend!

My army of mainly Britain's lead soldiers complete with Bren gun carriers, howitzers, field guns etc. led by Dinky toy tanks and anti-tank guns (not the same scale!) were constantly battling away. Strange to think that nowadays just one of the gas-masked soldiers will fetch £5 in good condition. I sold the whole army for £3 before I went to Dartmouth.

The Portsmouth Northern Secondary School had some excellent masters at this time. The Headmaster was Mr Hancock, Latin was taught by Mr Bradshaw (he was also very musical), and Mr Johns taught French. He was an expert stamp collector and traded stamps for a charity. Teachers really taught in those days and appeared to enjoy this demanding work. My brother, being four years older than me, was in the sixth form and a prefect. He gained a major scholarship to Queens' College at Cambridge in addition to a State Scholarship by virtue of his Higher School Certificate results. He got three distinctions but only a pass in Maths! He went on to gain a First Class honours degree in Biochemistry.

We went back to Portsmouth for the school holidays and of course by 1942–43 things were much quieter down south!

I was to spend much of 1943 swotting for the Common Entrance exam but at the time I did not realize what it would all lead to!

CHAPTER 2

Joining the Royal Navy – Cadet – Training Cruiser

1943 to Jan 1944: joining the Navy

I REALLY CANNOT BE CERTAIN exactly why I decided to join the Navy by going to Dartmouth. Being born and bred in Portsmouth, which was a major Naval Port, probably provided the major urge. It was A.V. Alexander, a Labour Naval Minister during the war, who enabled scholarships to be won at Dartmouth. A Portsmouth boy who had gone to Mile End House School, a small private school rather like Chivers where I had spent the early part of the war, had just won a scholarship to Dartmouth so I went round to see him to find out about it all. At that time Gieves, the naval tailors, published a small blue book called 'How to become a Naval Officer'. The first hurdle was of course the exam, which was the Common Entrance Exam used at that time by public schools to decide if their would-be pupils were fit to join them. My school was then evacuated to Winchester so I managed to get some old Common Entrance papers and made a list of the things I had to learn, particularly in the English and History papers. My History was really weak as the questions were about things I had not been taught. Maths was no problem. I cannot remember whether there were other subjects in my examination.

At any rate I passed the exam and rated an interview at Worcester College Oxford in November 1943. I was then 13 and faced an examination board comprising a rather deaf admiral, another senior naval officer, a headmaster and psychologist across the table from me. We had had to write an essay just beforehand to say which kind of ship we wanted to serve in at sea. I chose destroyers as they seemed very dashing and I had a book about them at home. I was questioned about this hurriedly written essay and then asked about my hobbies etc. Chemistry was actually my main hobby at that time. I think they thought I was talking about Lotts Chemistry sets and I

The author as a cadet at Royal Naval College

did enjoy telling them about my last experiment, which was from one of my brother's organic chemistry books, which involved a retort, and passing a gas over a heated substance. That took them back a bit, as there was no scientist there. Questions were fired at me by the admiral who had notices in front of him that read 'Speak up!', 'Speak louder!', 'How do you find the pole star?', 'What is a million?' I cannot remember how long the grilling went on but it seemed to go OK.

Then off to the medical examination, which was serious stuff! Every last crevice was explored. Every sense was tested. I had a bit of a set-to with the eye man who was establishing whether one was colour blind, obviously I was not but when we came to his signal lantern with coloured lights we had a difference of opinion about signal green! I think I kept saying blue (which it was actually), but he got a bit shirty with this idiot before him! A brace of doctors looked at my upper lip as I had been born with a near harelip and had a scar there. I had to say poetry etc. to persuade them that all was well and that I was normal. The real problem was that I had a roaring temperature that day with a bout of flu coming!

My father and I were put up at Campion Hall, a religious training college for the Roman Catholic Church. I do remember being given a half-pint glass of beer at supper that night more by accident than design and not knowing what I should do. I did not taste it but went to bed early as it had been a long day.

Later a letter in the post indicated that I would have been offered a place at Dartmouth but as I had suffered from a high temperature they had to be assured that I was now fit. So I hurried off to our local doctor for his OK! This was wafted off to the Admiralty and then a letter came through saying I was to be accepted as a cadet. Next, a trip to Gieves, which was then operating in the ground floor of an old hotel in Southsea, to be kitted up. This was quite something in wartime, when clothes rationing was the order of the day! We were to be provided with absolutely everything from top to bottom. There seemed to be an endless list with trunk and suitcase as well as all the clothes and uniform needed. It was all very exciting. Apart from all the uniform items there were sports kit, towels, stockings and even a large blue rug, which I still have.

In those days Dartmouth had been evacuated to Eaton Hall at Chester. So I travelled up to London, accompanied by my father, to join the special train; the trunk went ahead. Once I was parked on the train to Chester I was on my own like lots of others. On arrival at Eaton Hall new cadets joined Drake House for the first two terms. After that we went to our house assigned by that of our Tutor. My tutor was Mr Eustace and Hawk House it was to be. Naturally Drakes were the lowest of the low and that was why we started off in the main building to soften the blow before we went to Nissen huts.

January 1944 to August 1947: The Royal Naval College

In my time the Royal Naval College was run like a rather strict public school except that naval subjects were added to the curriculum at the expense of academic ones. As it was wartime many of the teaching Staff were old, although the naval officers were from the Active list. By the time I left the 'House Officers' were much decorated from their war service.

There were some 490 cadets proper who joined at the age of 13 plus and left after 11 terms at age 17. There were 57 Special Entry Cadets who spent two terms at the College before joining up with the ex-eleventh term cadets in the Training Cruiser. They were aged 17 or so on joining the Navy. We always regarded them as much older! They came from public school and grammar school sixth forms.

I found it surprising to literally go backwards in academic subjects in my first few terms. Although I was not yet 14 I was not at all overawed on joining the College now evacuated to Chester. The College returned to Dartmouth in 1946. I suppose that after several years of the war and having been bombed and evacuated life was just full of new exploits. The routine was like any well-oiled machine, slick and well rehearsed. We novices were soon marching correctly, doubling everywhere (one had to be very senior to walk!) and saluting Officers and the Quarterdeck.

There was no snobbery about the place. I had not been to a prep school or indeed a public school but soon made friends. There was just a little teasing about a Portsmouth accent, which I soon lost in this rarefied atmosphere.

History, apart from naval history, was not at all well taught. This was a pity as it was a favourite subject of mine. In later years it became almost a hobby, particularly military history. Modern history never figured in my time at Dartmouth. Modern language teaching is now far more productive than then, and much time was spent on learning by rote. I can still remember snippets from 'Conversations en Classe'.

We became dab hands at knots and splices, semaphore and morse. During several terms we spent a week doing 'engineering'. This ranged from fitting, which was mostly filing a spanner as far as I can remember, through carpentry, lathe work, welding and foundry work. I did succeed in directing the welding torch onto my other hand as I examined my task but fortunately the oxygen was turned off so the burns were minor! I had the distinct impression after these

Weekday Divisions at Eaton Hall

weeks that I was not cut out to be an engineer. Perhaps this was because the instruction was often sketchy and we dived in at the deep end. In later life I became quite a Do-It-Yourselfer, in spite of my early problems!

We doubled everywhere until we were seniors. There were all sorts of minor rules which had to be strictly obeyed, e.g. a white scarf had to be worn with a reefer jacket if wearing an open neck sports shirt. The pockets of reefer jackets were sewn up. In normal daywear a lanyard was worn strung between the lapels of the reefer jacket. The size of the bight between the lapels was determined by one's seniority so a Drake had it straight across and by the eleventh term it was almost down to the belly button!

There was plenty of sport: rugger in the autumn term, soccer and hockey in winter, cricket and tennis in summer. Athletics in the summer with standards to be achieved to gain points as well as races and competing to gain medals. In my senior term we won the Senior Gig race and I was 'pulling' on one of the central 16ft-long ash oars. Training was similar to that in a concentration camp and we were much relieved when it was all over! I was never much good or enthusiastic about sailing! Later in life, when asked if I sailed I always used to say 'only professionally'. I am sure that 'to sail' could enhance one's career prospects! On the one occasion a group of us went out for two days in one of the 'windfall yachts', so called as they had been taken from the Germans at the end of the war, we failed to get past Start Point. The wind and tide had prevented making much headway so we had to turn back. I remember eating a banana before seasickness took over. When we anchored that night we had a splendid meal and slept soundly. Dinghy sailing was a bit of a religion for some and the ability to use the wind and tide in the river Dart during sailing races became a fetish. This was just not my cup of tea.

I remember being concussed twice! Once during boxing when I came to in the changing room after a blow to the jaw and I had boxed on by reflex action and then walked to the changing room completely out! On the second occasion I played most of the second half of a game of rugger before I recovered my full senses in the dressing room.

Girls were something to be avoided at all costs! We learnt to dance on the Quarterdeck dancing with each other! No one thought this rather strange. Indeed it was not until my senior term that I went into Town (Dartmouth) by myself. Cadets were rather like a protected species and we were moulded very carefully into naval officers. We were soaked in tradition at an early age and taught much naval history. Obedience to orders had to be instant and unquestioning. Rules were rules no matter how puerile they might appear in later life. In this all male environment we knew little about girls and this need to learn about the opposite sex was well illustrated in the Training Cruiser. The Special Entry cadets who joined up with us then were much better versed in the ways of the world!

In our eighth term, if considered suited, we went to Alpha groups for more extensive teaching in Maths, Science, and Literary or Modern Languages. I went to the Russian Alpha. Our term was not thought to be sufficiently good to have a Maths Alpha although this did include science. I put this down to the appalling mathematics instruction we received up to then. I had always been quite good at maths but once we got to calculus and solid geometry all became a mystery. Alpha Classes spent more teaching periods in their chosen subject than the cadets did in what was known as Division 2.

Cadet Captains 11th term 1947

Unfortunately this meant that I had to give up History. I showed my mettle by winning the Graham Naval History Prize in my ninth term. This was a voluntary exam with a subject chosen by the College. The prize was three guineas-worth of books.

The Russian Alpha Class was taught by Count Nicholas Sollohub. He was a real Russian Count, his family having left Russia with the arrival of the Communists as many aristocratic families did. I must take my hat off to Mr de la Perrelle, who was Head of the Modern Language Department yet taught himself Russian so that he could teach this difficult language to those of us who wished to change from French, prior to selection for Alpha Class.

In the senior year, the ninth, tenth and eleventh terms, we could be selected for elevation to Cadet Captain. I managed this in my eleventh term. There were also House Cadet Captains like the Head of House at school and Chief Cadet Captains equivalent to Head of School. The only snag about this elevated living was that once you left Dartmouth you were right back to the lowest level. Cadet Captains being the equivalent of prefects in a school had privileges and were entitled to wear wing collars in formal uniform. This was felt to be very dashing.

Each House gave a play in the winter term. I appeared in two in a very minor role but I did get a taste for appearing on stage!

Our pocket money was one shilling a week and we were allowed a bank of five shillings at the start of term, which could be drawn against on request. We dutifully lined up on payday each week ready to accept our princely sum. I had a scholarship so the Admiralty paid my shilling, otherwise a cadet's parents paid it. Cadet Captains were paid an extra shilling (riches)!

I passed out First in my term so gained the King's Gold Medal and the Robert Roxburgh Prize, which was converted into a sword.

September 1947 to April 1948: Training Cruiser

The transition from Dartmouth to HMS *Devonshire*, the Training Cruiser, was quite a step change. We could smoke, go ashore, drink and meet girls as well as have some spare time and get paid!

I was now a seagoing cadet. We formed the working seamen crew of the ship and scrubbed decks, washed the paintwork, acted as boat's crews, cable party, berthing parties, and indeed anything expected of a seaman. We slept in hammocks on our messdeck and they were slung close together as was normal in ships then.

The autumn cruise went via Bantry Bay in South Ireland to Gibraltar, Ajaccio, Oran and Malta. Ajaccio was incredible, to be able to see Napoleon's birthplace and snorkel in clear blue sea to examine hordes of colourful fish was amazing. Furthermore, we could take soap and chocolate ashore to exchange for hard cash! We soon became spivs. These luxuries were in very short supply so soon after the war in French territory.

The winter cruise was to the West Indies with Barbados as the first stop and thence to Trinidad, Grenada, Antigua and Jamaica. At Jamaica we had to load up with the Gloucester Regiment and rush off to Belize as Guatemala was threatening invasion. This never happened but the scare did shorten our stay in the West Indies. The Myrtle Bank Hotel in Jamaica was a millionaire's paradise. We played golf at the Liguanea Club inside the Kingston Race Course. At Antigua we played golf against a local team. This was the first

Training Cruiser, HMS Devonshire, *trooping the Gloucesters to Belize*

and only course where I have played which possessed a par six hole because of the terrain.

I got badly sunburnt at Barbados when we were beaching a whaler to scrub it out in the brilliant sunshine, no one warned us of the likelihood of extreme sunburn as we spent some hours up to our waists in the sea by the beach. This ultimately gave me prickly heat, which I suffered from for years afterwards in hot climates. It was to be many years before I again visited the West Indies!

We had exams on the homeward trip and I was glad to have scraped a First Class pass. My boatwork in the Training Cruiser was not good mainly because no one ever taught me. I had to wait until I was a midshipman before I really got the hang of motorboats and the 'kitchen rudder gear' then widely used.

After leave we became midshipmen and did a month's Gunnery Course at HMS *Drake* at Devonport living onboard the Battleship *Vanguard*. We learnt to be Midshipman of the Watch on *Vanguard*'s quarterdeck where it was a goodly step to get from the port gangway to the starboard. The then Commander, Dreyer, was an excellent officer and became an Admiral. He was very kind to us makey-learn officers.

HMS Vanguard, *Gunnery Course 1948*

One night one of the midshipmen had a bright idea. It was to give a nickname to each of us on the letter rack bearing our names. I was given the name of Sam Snead the famous golfer because of my love of golf. Sam it has been ever since, although my mother and brother did not conform!

Plymouth was great fun with golf at Yelverton and steak, egg and chips very cheap in Union Street. Then off to our ships. A group of us were to go the Far East in the Troopship *Lancashire*.

CHAPTER 3

Midshipman, passage to Far East and HMS *London*

1948: Midshipman passage to Far East

I JOINED THE TROOPSHIP *LANCASHIRE* at Liverpool on Friday 25 June 1948 at 2 p.m. and we sailed that evening at 6 p.m. *Lancashire* was a very old Bibby Line Liner completed in 1917 and had been a troopship since 1931 and was due to be scrapped in 1939!

We midshipmen were accommodated on D deck. It was a very hot place and rather airless! We managed to while away the long passage with lectures, games and sleep. The only stop that I remember was a short one in Colombo, which gave me a chance to see the Gardens there and sample a drink at the best hotel, The Grand Oriental.

We arrived at Hong Kong on 28 July. This was not a moment too soon. Although the passage had not been too dull sleeping was always a problem in the confines of D deck and it was not a good place to be with my prickly heat!

On arrival we learnt that the Fleet was in Japan so we were to be accommodated in Stonecutters Island, eventually in tents, but to start with in the dining hall. We had five midshipmen to a tent and there were 15 of us in all. In its prime, say 1910, Stonecutters was an important place. There were old army barracks, quarters and gun emplacements. Now there was a wireless transmitting station, rifle range, obstacle and assault courses and the Royal Naval Armament Depot. The marines there taught us a lot about rifles, maintenance and sights. Life continued with swimming, as there was a beach and diving raft, cricket on a mat pitch and a little tennis. Life on the island was really close to nature. There were plenty of insects and the odd snake. We referred to the jungle near the tents as krait corner and it was probably true as a 5ft cobra was found and killed in the main block of tents!

Troopship Lancashire *1948*

Unfortunately I did not do any range firing as I developed a bad case of 'Hong Kong ear' and went to the Royal Naval hospital. There I had nitric acid wicks put in my ears. At the same time I had cysts removed from each of my eyelids. A few days in hospital were much appreciated for the comfy bed. I met up with my fellow midshipmen due to join *London* in HMS *Tamar*, the shore base in Hong Kong. We assembled our gear before joining HMS *Concord* on 18 August to sail for Japan.

Concord was built in 1946. C class destroyers were very handy ships of a 1944 design armed with four single 4.5-inch guns, one twin and two single Bofors, two Oerlikons and torpedo tubes in a quadruple mounting. In wartime the single 4.5-inch would be twin, there would be an increased AA armament and another quadruple torpedo mounting.

When we hitched our lift there were eight of us midshipmen and another eight officers taking passage, so she was a bit crowded. We kept four complete watches on the bridge during our trip. In talking to the ship's officers I gained the distinct impression that specialization required a much greater depth of knowledge and many preferred to remain unspecialized as 'salt horses'. They would always be needed at sea whereas the specialists spent quite a lot of time ashore.

The Captain of *Concord* gave us a short but very valuable talk about the Far East Station. He emphasized the need to get to know every place we visited and not just to inhabit the local club. It was a much better station for Officers than Ratings so this called for plenty of organized sports, picnic parties etc.

On 24 August we arrived in Ominato Bay and transferred to *London*, the flagship of the C-in-C Pacific Fleet. One of us was leaning over the side watching his gear being loaded when a voice behind asked if he had a good trip. On turning round he found himself face to face with Admiral Boyd, the C-in-C.

1948–49: HMS *London*

I do not think that there can have been a better and happier place to learn your trade than as a midshipman in a flagship in the Far East. We had all the excitement of places like Hong Kong, Singapore and Shanghai as well as visiting small coastal villages on the Malayan coast. There were naval ships from the USA, France, Australia and even Canada on this station. There was plenty of sport; we played rugger in Singapore and Shanghai mostly. There was plenty of swimming. Golf at the Island Club at Singapore, Fanling in Hong Kong and even at Shanghai. Squash at Singapore and Hong Kong. We met lots of people in the ports we visited and there were plenty of pretty girls to take dancing! At Trengganu a Saturday night dance in the local club saw the midshipmen dancing with the wives whilst their husbands celebrated with lots of 'stingahs' (whisky and soda). They kept us topped up to ensure that we continued to amuse their wives whilst they got on with the serious business!

We midshipmen learnt to accept responsibility at an early age by being in charge of a boat in all sorts of places and conditions. I was a midshipman in charge of a pinnace for a long time. We worked alternate days of duty when in harbour, often landing on open beaches on the Malayan coast or picking up drunks in Hong Kong or Singapore. One night we acted as long-stop to the MFV taking the sailors back to the ship in Singapore harbour, picking up the drunks as they fell or dived overboard!

It was always advisable to have a few friends among the sailors especially if things were to get fraught. The Coxswain of my pinnace was a tough chap, very experienced and would stand no nonsense, which helped especially with a load of very happy sailors

HMS London – *the 'lovely'* London

late at night. It was standard practice not to go alongside the ship to disembark until they quietened down. A marine butcher was a great friend and he would always ensure good behaviour in the boat.

It proved very important to be able to hold one's liquor. My sternsheetsman and the Royal Marine butcher took me on a 'run ashore' in Kowloon one night and we consumed an awful lot of rum during the evening. Eventually I left them and made my way back to the ship. Quite how I managed to climb the accommodation ladder I do not know because County Class Cruisers were quite large and it was a long way up the ladder. I could taste rum for days afterwards!

The American sailor was not very good at holding his drink and when a US ship came into Hong Kong and liberty guys were landed at noon or later, there were plenty of 'corpses' on the jetty by 4 o'clock and sometimes we assisted in carting them back to their ship.

American ships are 'dry', no liquor. That at least was the idea. When we visited an American cruiser and were looked after by the Ensigns they each had a small safe containing a bottle of bourbon. The tooth glasses were put to good use!

One excellent and memorable party was the Trooping of the Colour by the Buffs in Hong Kong. After the spectacle there was a cocktail party catered for by the 'Dairy Farm', an organization that ran the only (then) air-conditioned milk bar in Hong Kong. We were plied with endless 'White Ladies', an ice-cold concoction of gin, cointreau and lemon juice. It is seemingly quite harmless but actually lethal. One of our number went back happily to the ship and mistakenly carried on the party in the Warrant Officers' Mess drinking 'Green Dragons', a mixture of brandy and green chartreuse, also well iced. This was not a good idea and he got 'beaten' by the 'Snotties' Nurse' (the Lieutenant Commander assigned to look after the Midshipmen, who were often referred to as snotties) with a cane!

Every gunroom prided itself on the trophies it could exhibit. These could be things appropriated from other ships or from ashore, such things as name plates, street signs, barber's poles etc. It was the done thing. Nowadays this would be called vandalism but the top echelons tolerated it as long as you did not get caught. Thus it was an exercise in subterfuge, camouflage and taste!

The gunroom was run just like the wardroom with the Sub Lieutenant as the Mess President. We had mess dinners dressed up in white mess jacket and bow tie with cummerbunds. Officers from the ship were invited and one night the Commander and his No. 2 representing the Commander's Office (where the ship was run from) were our guests. It was customary to have the guests wind their way through the pipe work in the ceiling of the gunroom after dinner. The Commander was quite beefy and relied on his assistant to coax him through the narrow gaps to the applause of the midshipmen.

When reading through my journal I realize how often the boat broke down! My pinnace time was continually interrupted with engine failures of one sort or another, even then this was not the end of problems as the exhaust system blew a hole and started to flood up the engine. The motor boats and the pinnaces were then fitted with what was known as 'kitchen rudder gear'. Two buckets surrounded the propeller and by winding them open one way or the other determined whether the boat went ahead or astern. The more open the buckets the more speed generated. The handwheel to open the buckets was situated on the helm and you had to be adept at doing two things at once. This device did allow excellent control of the boat though and with practice you could become quite expert.

Eventually I changed to driving a motorboat and this meant that my passengers would be officers. One night after the Sunday film show we were waiting alongside the gangway to take officers' guests back to Stonecutters Island when a large black rat was spotted in the boat. We could not catch it so the ladies in their evening dresses shared the boat's cabin with this rat and we had to hope that they would never know.

One lesson that we would later never forget was the effect of the tide. A heavily laden pinnace with the tide behind would never ever stop and sailed past the intended disembarkation point. Cutters propelled by ratings with oars were used to assist the ship securing to buoys. Once again the tide fooled me and the cutter sailed past the buoy resulting in a long wait until the ship was again in position for the 'picking up rope' to be passed and secured to the buoy. In the boat I could imagine the castigation going on up top and on the bridge. Unfortunately on this occasion my cutter's crew were not as experienced as before. Much later on I did make amends with a very smart securing to the buoy.

It was after my disaster with the tide that I foolishly steadied myself when the boat was being hoisted by holding on to the fall (the rope going through the block at one end of the boat and being used to hoist the boat). So my fingers started to go through the block with the rope. I pulled out my fingers but my right index finger was a bit squashed and bleeding profusely. So it had to be stitched up and this meant that I was not able to be much use for a few weeks! I always blame this incident for the bad handwriting I now have!

Because of the situation in China there was a steady stream of American ships in Hong Kong at this time and of course also in Shanghai. The Americans had a base in Tsingtao, which they were going to evacuate. They did also have many bases in Japan and elsewhere. The US cruisers were armed with 6-inch and 5-inch guns but had no armour. I noted how very clean they were inside and that a vacuum cleaner was all that was needed between decks, unlike our cleanliness problems! The interior was very warlike with fire hazards kept to a minimum thus giving a very bare look.

During our trips to Shanghai we soon got to appreciate inflation. During our first visit the theoretical exchange rate was 12 gold yuan to the Hong Kong dollar. By the time we left it was a 1000. Eventually it was to be 4 million to the US dollar! Increasing inflation suited us very well as we could run up a bill at the French Club situated in the French enclave in Shanghai and pay for it much later with gold yuan obtained at the newest exchange rate.

The ship's refit in Singapore meant that we had to live ashore in the naval barracks, HMS *Terror*. We midshipmen were put in double cabins and luxuriated with a bed each.

This happy existence gave us a chance to play plenty of sport – rugger, hockey, squash and golf. Golf at the Island Club cost 2 Singapore dollars a round but fortunately we received £10 tropical uniform allowance, which was spent on other things, so some of us joined the golf club for a month for 12 dollars. We were always short of cash and on many occasions payday was eagerly awaited as the bank account was bare and the wine bill almost expended.

The Commander in Chief invited the midshipmen in groups for a four-day stay at Admiralty House in Singapore city. This was real luxury as we were driven to the Tanglin Club in the Admiral's Rolls Royce complete with marine driver. There we played tennis and swam. The admiral's daughter named Bushie, although older than us, was great fun and looked after us. It was a very happy time full of memories and even included a game of golf with the C-in-C and his Flag Lieutenant at the Royal Singapore Golf Club.

Apart from boat-running the midshipmen did plenty of watch-keeping on the Quarterdeck in harbour. This involved much ceremonial, especially as we were a flagship. There was plenty of 'piping the side' for admirals, captains of ships, and foreign officers. The routines of the ship and the boats occupied us, as the timetable was very important. Also we had to attend to seamanlike matters such as sloping the awnings when it rained, and did it rain! I often cursed the weather when wearing full whites in Singapore whilst paddling around the deck!

Throughout our time as midshipmen we were doing a course of study on all the subjects that would be tested during our 'Board', the examination we had to take at the end of our midshipmen's time before promotion to Sub Lieutenant. We learnt about electrics, which were very basic then, gunnery, torpedoes, communications, supply duties, general administration and engineering. The engineering course lasted for a month and we spent days touring the bowels of the ship. Engineering watchkeeping experience in the boiler room and engine room was very boring, noisy and hot. It is one of my boasts that I have been inside a turbine, having negotiated the small access hole. Boiler cleaning was another pastime that I would never describe as thrilling.

Because of the situation in China there were a number of exercises in the New Territories testing procedures for the army in defending the area including bombardment by ships. I did two exercises attached to the army with the FOBs (Forward Observer Bombardment). The army food was awful! Although on one night the army regiment had a dinner in their tent with the mess silver and all mod cons! On another night we paused at the army barracks for a cocktail party. The naval contingent attended in fighting rig complete with boots and khaki anklets whilst the army were in some very fancy mess dress! On the first exercise we had no tents or shelter of any sort and ended up sleeping in the rain under a lorry and then in the cab. Next time we were better prepared and even had our own transport. The Navy were not very warlike as we wore caps with white capcovers on the hilltops.

I never really understood how the Canadian destroyer *Crescent* ended up in Shanghai but two lucky midshipmen got a ride in her up to Nanking. Canadian beer was much stronger than our canned beer and was very, very good.

We spent Christmas 1948 in Shanghai and had quite a long stay that time. The world famed Shanghai Club, which then had the longest bar in the world, had the main part of the bar in darkness as these were troubled times. The French Club in the Avenue Joffre was a splendid retreat with good food, bar and dancing but the curfew meant that we had to be back onboard quite early. This was just as well as Shanghai was a dangerous place to be late at night and one or two American sailors were knifed. We played rugger on the pitch at the Shanghai racecourse, where it was very strange to hear a commentary over the loudspeakers given by an American whilst we were playing!

Later on, in March 1949, the local Chinese general gave a dinner. It was very large gathering and included our sailors. It was a typical Chinese banquet with lots of tasty courses and plenty of yam sing (bottoms up!) with rice wine. This very festive occasion was held in the Police Club, rather like fiddling whilst Rome burned, as we were soon to have demonstrated in the Yangtze.

It is interesting to note that the ex-pats in Hong Kong and Singapore seldom, if ever, invited sailors or for that matter officers to their homes. This was particularly evident in Singapore where the Old Raj reigned supreme. I found this strange and really unforgivable, as the people there whom we were to protect if required just ignored the Services. It was a different story in Shanghai where the Communists were not far away!

After our return from the Yangtze incident (see p26) to Hong Kong we each had 48 hours leave and I was lucky to find myself in a beach hut in Middle Bay with Peter Coulson, a mate from the gunroom. This was owned by the local Methodist Minister and Peter was friendly with the daughter (I believe he married her eventually). We had a splendid couple of days on the beach with a plentiful supply of brandy.

My journal records many of the important features of life back in the UK in 1948-9. There was devaluation, the Dock strike, Berlin airlift and so on. The birth of Prince Charles resulted in 'Splice the Mainbrace', but not for us midshipmen, and we had to be content with a glass of limejuice!

Towards the end of *London*'s time in the Far East the ship went to north Borneo, visiting Jesselton and Sandakan. Both of these were small out of the way places. You could see the value of such visits right away. Beat Retreat, with the Royal Marine band, was always a heart-warming affair and I am sure that the locals would remember it for many a long year. Also they had the chance to go onboard one of HM warships. After this we went to Khota Bharu and Trengganu on the east Malayan coast. The showing of the flag there was equally valuable. It is a pity that our shrinking navy cannot carry out this valuable ambassadorial duty like it used to. Our politicians seem to have no appreciation of history and the wealth of experience this country has acquired. Consequently they have frittered away billions of pounds and cut the armed forces to shreds in the interest of economy! One day we may well regret this downward path.

As the time for our Midshipman's Board approached we had a dummy Board run by Ship's officers including the Captain and the

Commander. This was a very necessary exercise as it exposed a few gaps in our knowledge, particularly in seamanship.

When the real Board came along we were much better prepared. I managed to gain a First Class pass although I did have a tangle with the Captain, who was president of Board, on the subject of man overboard. I remember that I did not like him or his attitude to me as a candidate; this did not help my marks from him. Later in life I was to be the President of many Boards for RNR officers, seeking to gain their watchkeeping certificate. I took some pride in my way of using the time to have a bit of a 'teach in' with each candidate. I think this was appreciated.

So *London* headed homewards and we were sporting a nice gold stripe as Acting Sub Lieutenants.

It is a great pity that so much emphasis is placed on university degrees these days. There is no substitute for the University of Life! There was a television programme about the Royal Naval College at Dartmouth several years ago when the would-be naval officers were much older than in my day. The graduates were making a hash of one of the leadership problems being set nowadays. They had to construct a raft from oil drums, timber and ropes to cross a stream. Their Royal Marine Officer instructor faced the camera with his beret badge at full face saying 'I have found that the common sense in any group is in inverse proportion to the degrees held by them'! My generation of naval officers was indeed fortunate to have learnt our trade from an early age at sea from professionals.

The Yangtze Incident

Extract from the Midshipman's Journal

WEEK ENDING APRIL 23 1949
    I was on the bridge at 1000 a.m. when a Flash signal was received from HMS *Amethyst*. It read 'Am aground under heavy fire in position . . . .large number of casualties'. No more signals came through. This naturally had serious implications. After Stand Easy the Commander cleared Lower Deck and addressed the Ship's Company telling them of the situation. We then cleared for Action, furling awnings etc. Eight-inch shell was fused. Four-inch practice ammunition was removed from the ready use lockers and they were filled with live ammunition. Close range ammunition was got up on deck. Pom-pom belts were filled and Oerlikon magazines loaded.

Amethyst had been on her way from Shanghai to Nanking and was relieving HMS *Consort*, who was standing by British nationals there. She had come under fire from Communist batteries on the north bank and also small arms fire. The Coxswain was killed and slumped on the wheel. This unfortunately grounded the ship. In this position she came under heavy fire. A and B guns were useless and owing to heavy fire it was impossible to man X and Y and give aid to the seriously wounded. Both the doctor and the SBA were killed early in the action. The Captain was seriously wounded and later died from his wounds. Casualties were heavy, morphia was badly needed. There she lay in a crippled condition. She was actually grounded near Rose Island.

At 1130 we picked up the pilot at the Yangtze entrance and later increased speed to 20 knots when the depth of water increased.

Meanwhile HMS *Black Swan* was dispatched from Shanghai and HMS *Consort* from Nanking. At 1415 we anchored off Woosung picking up two Chinese pilots for the Yangtze and a British pilot. The Assistant Naval Attaché, Commander Pringle, came onboard to talk to the Admiral and he left before we got underway again at 1520.

Yangtze River.

Events Concerning H.M.S. London, Consort, Black Swan.
April 20-21st 1949.

Map of Yangtze incident 1949

We went to Action Stations to test communications and get everyone happy and expectantly ready. Pom-poms were loaded, as were the eight-inch hoists. By this time signals had been received from HMS *Consort*. One at 1300 reported small arms fire when she was still some 20 miles from *Amethyst*. On reaching the *Amethyst* she encountered fire and turned back in order that she might tow her off. She received heavy fire and *Amethyst* told her to go while the going was good. She received hits in the TS, Wheelhouse and Bridge Wireless Office. Several were killed and there were many seriously wounded. The bridge received flying shrapnel and the Captain was wounded in the leg.

She had two of her 4.5-inch guns put out of action; A gun had an anti-tank shell through its barrel. B gun received a direct hit killing many of its crew. She had a large hole forr'd on the waterline. She had evidently been engaged with 105mm anti-tank guns. She was flying five ensigns and two jacks to make it clearly visible that she was British.

We heard that *Amethyst* was in a critical position with heavy casualties. The upper deck was untenable owing to heavy fire and she would have been unable to tend wires in any case. The situation seemed desperate and very tense.

The Captain informed the Ship's Company of the situation and said it was clearly our duty to go to the aid of *Amethyst*.

After falling out from Action Stations the Ship went to Special Cruising Stations with one eight inch turret manned, four close range guns and the pom-pom manned on the starboard side, that facing the north bank. Four-inch guns were split up into two watches, working watch and watch in the daytime only. The red watch had the last Dogwatch.

At 2010 we sighted HMS *Consort* and HMS *Black Swan* alongside each other at Kiangyin. At approximately 2100 we anchored at Kiangyin and *Black Swan* came alongside our starboard side followed by *Consort* on the port side. We began to embark *Consort*'s seriously wounded for treatment. Many of them had been badly burnt by flash and several were shell-shocked. She looked seriously damaged. Her wheelhouse was riddled, as was her bridge. She was steering from aft. We oiled both *Black Swan* and *Consort*, transferring provisions to *Consort*.

The situation was definitely critical. We sent repair parties to *Consort* to see what could be done. Her side needed some first aide and also her electrics needed attention. We were beginning to appreciate the situation far more fully. Everyone onboard was eager for action of some sort. They were spoiling to go to *Amethyst*'s aid. Hence we were destined to wait for the morrow with the Ship at special Cruising Stations.

With Wednesday as the deadline for peace with the Communists, this was the eve of the Communist D-day. The staff meeting onboard went on well into the night as great decisions had to be made, which were destined to have a serious bearing on our future.

I had the morning watch and sunrise found us in company with some Chinese Nationalist gunboats and a Nationalist bridgehead on the north bank. There was some activity on the north bank. *Consort* left to go to Shanghai with her wounded.

Before *Black Swan* slipped at 0605 and we weighed anchor a signal was received from *Amethyst*. She had managed to refloat. She was told to proceed further up river. Casualties were very heavy. Many of the Ship's Company had managed to get ashore including several of the wounded. This at least was heartening news. She had still encountered gunfire and small arms fire.

We came to anchor again at 0725 still some 30 miles from *Amethyst*. The decision to go on had to be made. This was known to be the Communist D-day, we were in a sticky position and it was a difficult decision to make. The Captain told us we were going on to the rescue of our shipmates. It is in my humble opinion the one and only course to take. Our object was to go up river and, together with *Black Swan*, escort *Amethyst* back. We had purely peaceful intentions. We prepared to tow aft, a rather ironical preparation. *Amethyst* had signalled that she could steer and was able to steam at her normal speed though.

At 1020 or so we weighed anchor and proceeded up river at Action Stations. We were flying a white flag, numerous jacks and a large 'battle' ensign. All this to show our peaceful intentions, but with little avail.

Black Swan followed us astern similarly 'dressed' overall. We had as many personnel as possible out of harm's way. Port guns crews were in safety and below decks, everyone laid low on the disengaged side. Men in exposed places had anti-flash gear on and wore tin helmets.

I was between decks when we opened fire as it was considered best to clear the GDP of all unnecessary people to lessen casualties.

At 1036 the Communist battery at Lin-wei-chiang opened fire. We downed the white flag and returned fire with everything we had got. The ship was hit in the hangar causing a fire there. B turret was hit on the side; the shell bounced and injured all the Bofors crew (L one). The ship's side was holed at the ERA's bathroom. By 1040 firing had ceased as we speeded up and passed the batteries. Strange as it may seem we rehoisted the white flag. This was part of our 'peace' policy.

We were again under fire soon after 1100 having passed *Amethyst's* empty whaler drifting downstream. The battery was at Kuo Ching Chiang and the white flag was down for good this time! At 1105 there was a direct hit on the bridge. The Chinese pilot was killed outright as the shell must have exploded on his helmet. The OOW and the PCO received slight shrapnel wounds. The Navigating Officer was seriously wounded and the Captain was also slightly wounded. Luckily the three midshipmen there escaped injury.

This caused the Captain to decide to turn the ship, as it was now obvious that if we reached *Amethyst* at this rate we would not be fit to do much escorting. Casualties were now becoming more and more and evidently the Communists were intent upon us not getting up river. Soon firing ceased on both sides as apparently their guns could not train on us and whilst turning we were in the shelter of Beaver Island. The ship turned to starboard and the Emergency conning position took control of the ship. Meanwhile we were lucky not to go aground as we were at one time heading towards the bank at 22 knots. *Black Swan* astern of us was on the point of preparing to tow us off!

At 1106 firing ceased on both sides and whilst the ship was turning the Commander took command. It was the Captain's decision to turn in face of heavy fire. By 1120 all was well on the bridge again but firing recommended at 1124 when the previous battery engaged us again. The Commander left the ECP and came forr'd to take over, assisted by the British pilot, Captain Sudbury. The Captain later left the bridge to have his wounds dressed.

By 1132 all firing had ceased but 5 minutes later the battery at Tien shen chiao engaged us. After a further period another battery at Tien shen chiao engaged the ship. Later at 1152 the Liu-wein chiang battery opened up. The Captain was on the bridge again at 1215 after a short period below. At 1245 a battery to the west of Pa wei chieang fired, this proved to be heavy and took its toll. By 1257 firing had ceased. There was a temporary lull and we had Action messing-tiddy oggies, apples and oranges while Action Stations was temporarily relaxed. The Captain said over the warning telephone that he hoped we were clear but unfortunately this was completely untrue.

At 1330 the ship returned fire from a battery near Hsin chiang. This was a costly action as four were killed on the four-inch gundeck, including one of my old coxswains of the pinnace – Leading Seaman Arkell, a sad loss. The four-inch gundeck had been converted into a charnel house. One of the ready use lockers caught fire and ammunition was getting dangerous so it was wisely dumped overboard. This was our last engagement and the other Chinese pilot was 'persuaded' to go to the bridge. He was in a very shaken condition and was not very useful. Meanwhile the Navigating Officer had been the British pilot, Captain Sudbury, aided by the Staff Operations Officer, Commander Hare.

At 1430 we were well clear of possible Communists and known danger areas so at 1500 we secured Action Stations and surveyed our damage. We began the sordid business of clearing up. The ship entered the Whangpoo at 1725 after picking up a pilot and secured alongside Holts Wharf. *Black Swan* berthed alongside us. It was certainly a most welcome sight. We came in with a band playing and a guard paraded. A crowning gesture!

As soon as possible our not so serious casualties were disembarked into American LCMs and rushed off to hospital in the Glen Line Building. It had been hoped that *Repose* (an American hospital ship) would be at Woosung. Her later presence was invaluable.

The more serious cases went later to USS *Repose* where everyone was concentrated in the long run. The Navigating officer was still alive and putting up a strong fight for his life although critically wounded.

Our casualties were now 12 killed and 15 others seriously wounded with a further 20 injured. *Consort* had suffered 10 dead and

15 seriously wounded. *Black Swan* had 5 seriously wounded. *Amethyst* 2 officers and 17 ratings killed and 3 officers and 21 ratings seriously wounded. These were the known casualties so far.

Black Swan had got away with fairly 'light' damage owing to us presenting a bigger target and drawing the main part of the fire. She was, however, holed in the port oil fuel tanks. Naturally she had been able to dodge some of the fire she encountered. Our damage was as follows. Communist fire had been concentrated at first in the fore part of the ship. The bridge superstructure and below received heavy punishment. Later the four-inch gundeck became a scene of heavy damage. Much of our damage was encountered on the way back. On the port side of the ship there were a score of holes. Several shells had 'bounced' and not penetrated, proving she was still pretty tough.

The fire encountered was from 105 mm and 40 mm guns, the latter with armour-piercing heads. Opinion has it that there may have been some 125 mm but this is doubtful. I do not think that we encountered small arms fire because of the range. When we emerged from action the four-inch guns on the port side were in local control. X turret was the only one in action. Half of our close

HMS London, *shellfire damage, Yangtze incident 1949*

range weapons were functioning. Attempts had been made to get Y turret in action but this was too late to be of any use.

The following received the main hits – B shell handling space, starboard hangar, schoolroom, information room, old gunroom bathroom, ERA's bathroom, Capstan flat (canvas store), PO's bathroom, Stokers, Lambeth and watchkeeper's messdecks. A and B turrets were hit and the eight-inch Director was hit at least three times, shattering the aerial. Several guns were damaged and there was much damage around the four-inch gundeck. W/T aerials were shot away. Electrics all over the ship were disorganized, cut or blown away. Several communication systems were put out of action. Considerable damage was sustained elsewhere. It would be impossible to recount all our damage.

Casualties were sustained all over the ship. Many resulted on the four-inch gundeck, which besides being exposed came in for a heavy proportion of shells and resulting shrapnel. Two were killed outright in the B shell handling space. Four were killed around a 15-cwt truck during the last action. This truck had given shelter to many all the way through. Fate had it that it was to be hit though. So casualties mounted up all over the ship. I cannot say more.

We had actually given ourselves a list to starboard, which at one time was five degrees but later settled to three. This was to stop flooding from the hole at the waterline by the shell which ended up in B shell handling room. *Black Swan* had listed to port owing to flooding of her oil fuel tanks on that side. Immediate repairs were effected and welding was soon taking place.

To sum up, the whole object of our mission was to escort *Amethyst* downstream. It was purely and simply a matter of going to the aid of our 'fleetmates'. This was the only thing we could do. We were unsuccessful. We turned back as the casualties to be sustained would not justify our continuance up river. We were fortunate to have the Admiral and his staff onboard as they were able to appreciate the situation better than if they had been in Hong Kong.

Many of us were left asking 'Was it worth it?' Between us all we had more casualties than *Amethyst*. Yes, it was definitely worth it, we did our best and what was more we tried not to desert our fleetmates when they needed us. We may have waited until nightfall to fulfil our mission but not only would we have hazarded the ship's safety but have been too late. Delay was fatal. If the ship had gone aground the situation would have been disastrous. *Amethyst* was going up river on the 'eve' of D-day, which to the uninformed seemed slightly peculiar owing to intelligence reports which said it would be definitely risky. *Consort* could probably have stayed at Nanking but in the end the position was as stated.

Note

This was written in my journal soon after the Incident when I was 19 years old! The wording and grammar is exactly as written at the time and has not been changed.

CHAPTER 4

Sub Lieutenant's courses Greenwich, Portsmouth and Gosport

September 1949 to March 1950: Greenwich

IN SEPTEMBER 1949 I JOINED the Royal Naval College Greenwich for two terms.

I think the idea was to further our education by giving us a broader view of the world by having lectures from various luminaries, write essays on various subjects to test our ability to write and research a subject in the library, and even dabble in some science (chemistry).

We were paid very little, just 11 shillings a day (55p in today's money!) yet managed to smoke, drink and visit the odd London theatre as well as meet with the opposite sex! I remember one invitation to a Kensington Finishing school. The staff there must have been somewhat alarmed by the arrival of a band of us chaps.

I played a fair amount of rugger at Greenwich and quite often followed a bruising game on Saturday with golf on the Sunday morning. Therefore the golf was not exactly dynamic.

We were split into groups and had a group tutor from the academic staff. Mine was the naval padre, and I got along quite well with him and he let me off his lecture one day a week so that I could go off to London University for Serbo Croat lessons. I just played hooky from the chemistry on the other day. As I had studied Russian at Dartmouth another Slav language fascinated me. I also kept up with my Russian with a Doctor Colin who came to the college to teach Russian. He lived in some style in St Johns Wood. He took me to Cambridge to see a Russian play, putting me up at the Blue Boar there, then a nice little hotel, rather than a Berni Inn. He always travelled First Class and had a box in the theatre as he suffered from claustrophobia. I did manage to persuade him to come to *Thermopylae*'s commissioning party several years later and we stood him under the hatch so he could see the sky!

After a night on the town many Sub Lieutenants were not in prime condition to give our lecturers the attention they deserved and there were always many sleeping heads in the large lecture theatre.

Having only attended one chemistry period I still managed the exam with some judicious cheating from someone else's notes, although because chemistry had been my hobby in my younger days, there was no real problem.

I broke my ankle playing rugger against the London School of Economics at Kingston during a Saturday match. I was transported to the Accident and Emergency department of the local hospital where I shivered in my shirt and shorts whilst waiting for an X-ray and then for my ankle to be plastered. My injury seemed slight when I talked to a chap who had both his legs broken in a soccer tackle. Eventually I got back late in the day to Greenwich and made my way somehow to my cabin. Word must have got round to the sickbay as the CPO from there soon appeared saying I should have reported there. Little did he know how I felt at that time!

With my leg in plaster up to the knee I was rather imprisoned for the rest of the term. I do remember that my 'chums' pinched my crutches at the final mess dinner!

HMS Alderney *1950*

After Greenwich Sub Lieutenants did a 3-month spell at sea before starting their professional courses at the various schools in the Portsmouth area. I was due to go to a submarine at Fort Blockhouse at Gosport. But there I was, clad in plaster. I went to Haslar hospital to have my plaster taken off and persuaded the doctor there that I was fit by jumping up and down with my leg now encased in Elastoplast. It hurt but I made sure I did not show it! So off to sea in HMS *Alderney* for exercises, including 'Flag Officer Submarine's Summer war', the annual big exercise for the submarines of the home station.

August 1950 to May 1951: Portsmouth

Our term of Sub Lieutenants was divided into groups. Mine was Q group and for some unknown reason I was designated as the Group leader throughout our courses. There were 11 of us in the group and we were split 50/50 Special Entry and Ex Dartmouth cadets. We had a pretty happy time during our months together.

Our first course was to be the Electrical one at HMS *Collingwood*, then just a collection of Nissen huts! For some reason we started in August whilst all the rest of the term due to start courses at the various establishments were now on summer leave. Electrics then was a very dull and boring subject and quite why we had to examine the intricacies of a winch motor was totally beyond me. Three of the group failed this course. We had exams at the end of every course. I was taken aside and questioned about the group's performance. I do not believe I gave a very convincing answer!

After our summer leave we went to Lee on Solent for the Air Course during which we flew in many different aircraft. I remember flying upside down in a Meteor and the pilot saw me bouncing up and down on the canopy as I had come right out of my seat as I had not been properly strapped in. One evening I volunteered for a flight in a Firefly conducting torpedo attacks on ships in the Solent. Great fun zooming over at masthead height. However, flying was not for me! It was one of our pleasures to take the Link Trainer up to 20,000ft and put it into a spin which took it all the way down to earth in a spiral before 'crashing'. The real thing would not have been so much fun though.

The Torpedo and Anti Submarine Course at HMS *Vernon* was by far the most enjoyable of all the Courses. The greatest fun was taking a destroyer in to launch torpedoes at a German cruiser at a range of 1000 yards under intense 'shellfire' in the trainer, which had a replica destroyer bridge and torpedo sight in the centre of a cylindrical structure. The enemy Target was a projected image on the wall facing you and got steadily bigger as the range closed. We also experienced going down in a full diver's suit in a large tank of water.

I must give special mention to the Gunnery Course at HMS *Excellent*. It is scarcely credible that we were still expected to practise Company Drill in the 1950s. Company Drill was more in keeping with Naval Brigades in the Boer War rather than modern warfare. As Sub Lieutenants we each had a 'go' at being the Company Commander at Divisions on the parade ground. We were expected to detail the drill in best parade ground manner and then get them to do the rather complicated manoeuvre. Not really having much of a clue about the particular drill that I was lumbered with I gave the assembled company a loud harangue about what they were to do and then set it all in motion. At the end of a somewhat bedraggled affair I told them off in best Gunnery fashion, that is very loudly, for not doing it well. Afterwards I was congratulated on the 'telling off' even though my drill was completely wrong. When carrying out live firings at the Wembury Gunnery Range near Plymouth I was the Fuse Keeping Clock operator for our AA shoot and was dutifully following pointers as instructed in the drill. When the first shell was fired it exploded soon after leaving the barrel, much to everyone's consternation. I had been following pointers all the way down to zero! We also did live firings in a Battle Class Destroyer, HMS *Finisterre*. We fired practice shells at a towed target. On the firing day we disposed of some 200 practice shells. The Sub Lieutenants moved around all the positions like gunlayer, trainer, gunnery officer etc. I think most of us were pretty terrified and slightly deaf as the 4–inch gun makes a very painful crack to the ear and no one cared about Health and Safety regulations then! I suppose we thought we knew what was going on at the time!

Our Course officer at the Gunnery School at Whale Island was a Royal Marine Officer. In those far off days Marine Officers could qualify as Long Course Gunnery Officers. Our Marine was one of those very solid types and one afternoon after he had explained, in a most laborious manner, how the Gyro Rate Unit worked, one of our number virtually recapitulated the whole of what he had said and ended by saying that he still did not understand this wonderful piece of gadgetry. The Marine Officer stared at him in blank astonishment whilst we had a laugh!

Mess Dinners at Whale Island were great fun if not dangerous. After dinner it was customary to re-enact the Field Gun Competition with an Officer acting as the gun barrel and a sofa as the carriage. The route was through a single doorway and the gun's crew would fight their way through.

Courses in Combined Operations, Communications, Navigation, Divisional and Damage Control came and went. I managed a First Class Pass in each of my courses which meant a £10 prize of books and more importantly extra seniority as a Lieutenant as this guaranteed extra pay earlier than normal.

For us the Damage Control course was the last one and on the final day of our course was the examination. We were not very interested as the Sub Lieutenant's dance in London was to be held that evening. We were all keen to get away! The Sub Lieutenants' 1951 dance at 6 Stanhope Gate on Friday 18 May 1951 signified the end of courses. There was now the Submarine Training Class to come!

1951: Submarine Training Class Gosport

I cannot really say why I volunteered for submarines, possibly because surface ships did not appeal during our Sub Lieutenant's Courses. It was noteworthy that of the eight midshipmen of the same vintage as me in *London*'s gunroom four of us volunteered for Submarines. Also one of the three junior midshipmen and one of the two senior midshipmen were submarine volunteers. Perhaps we were inspired by Shorty Stoop who was in *London* as the Foretop Divisional Officer. Our Snotties' Nurse, Tommy Catlow, may have influenced us. I do know that he was very proud when he found out that so many of us were making a career in submarines.

Submarine Training Class

As midshipmen we did go onboard a submarine in Hong Kong whilst it was tied up alongside and painted green, the Far East colour scheme for British submarines then. The Mediterranean ones were a nice blue colour and in Home waters they were grey. Much later on all British submarines were painted black!

We had done a short trip out to sea in a T class boat whilst at Dartmouth and were very thankful when we dived. We had been parked in the stokers mess right aft during a rough passage to the Diving Area and felt very seasick, buckets were provided!

So I joined Officers' Training Class 119 in June 1951, the beginning of a long career in Boats. The previous class had been lost in the *Affray* so we had to make up for the serious loss of Officers due to join the Submarine Service. There were 16 of us, including two Electrical Officers, as the T Conversion class submarine was about to come into service and they required an Electrical Officer in their complement because of more advanced systems. The Mechanical Engineers had their own Training Class – and their previous one had gone down in the *Affray* as well.

Affray sank in the Channel whilst giving sea experience to both the Seamen Officers' and Engineer Officers' Training Classes. After a long and extensive search when nothing had been heard from her she was discovered in a deep trench with signs of damage to her snort mast. It was concluded after an Inquiry that she had sunk after a snorting accident. It was realized that it was a major mistake to have so many Officers under training onboard and steps were taken to ensure that this could not happen in the future.

The CO of the Submarine School was Rumble Clutterbuck, whom I remember as rather old before his time. Lance Bell Davies was the Officers' Training Officer, Chief Petty Officer Selby, a distinguished coxswain from the last war and one of the few survivors of his submarine when it sank off Malta having been mined – he swam a considerable distance to shore. He was obviously a very lucky man as he should have been onboard *Affray* but did not sail in her as he was sick at the time.

Submarine training has improved considerably since our time in tin huts at Blockhouse. Things had to improve in order to take in the growing complexity of submarines, their propulsion and weapons. Nowadays they have films, models, and trainers that perform like the real thing etc. We had lots of pictures, some hardware, and not a lot else. There were no handouts; you made your own notes and drawings of pipe systems etc. Now there is a nice printed notebook given to you complete with system diagrams and there are Training Aid Books describing each system in detail with coloured diagrams.

We were of course rather 'course happy' having just done nine months of Sub Lieutenant's courses. I had done three months in *Alderney* after the Greenwich course. Chimp Clayden was the Captain, Matty Todd the First Lieutenant, Zachary Bath the Engineer and Maurice Ingram the Navigator. Therefore I had a reasonable idea of what was required in spite of the lack of handouts. Some practical things were rather raced over so that we often only had a bit of the overall picture. During my oral exam at the end of the Course I produced a massive spark from the switchboard as I broke a switch without doing the correct thing with the 'field switch', much to my amazement and the horror of the examining officer! Our understanding of the workings of submarine radar was also just about as primitive as the radar itself. To be fair there were no courses about instructional technique in those days and all Naval instruction was not all it should have been!

In the days before the 100 ft tower was built and new methods of submarine escape widely installed, submarine escape training was conducted in a shallow tank using the Davis Escape Apparatus. Below about 30 feet this particular device was actually lethal as oxygen under pressure can kill. This was one of the outcomes of the *Truculent* enquiry after she sank in the Thames.

The new escape tower and immersion suit and later the use of the hood was a step change in submarine escape. The original research carried out in the Royal Naval Physiology lab in Gosport was taken up by the submarine service most enthusiastically and a succession of Officers in Charge of Submarine Escape Training have ensured that we lead the world with this equipment and training. It was very exciting coming up from 100ft secured to a central wire as leaning back acted as a hydroplane and the tether prevented you hitting the side of the tank so one just circled the central wire on the way up. Before the hooded suit the method was called 'Free Ascent' which meant breathing out continuously on the way up, otherwise the expanding air in the lungs would rupture them. If the instructors waiting in the tank at various depths did not see sufficient bubbles you got a hefty belt in the chest!

During submarine training we had a demonstration of the effects of being under pressure and also breathing too much oxygen. Trying to pick up ball bearings with tweezers being fully convinced of your capability when actually you are making a mess of it was most amusing for the onlookers.

I must now make a confession! I have to reveal that at the medical examination for entry into submarines, which we did on arrival at Fort Blockhouse, I cheated! My eyesight had been perfect but deteriorated as a midshipman, probably through the effects of tropical sunshine. It did mean that I could not really read the small letters required in the eye test with one of my eyes. I got one of my chums to learn the letters and when it was my turn I faltered with my good eye and went rapidly through the line with my bad one. No one ever rumbled this dodge throughout my service thank goodness. I must emphasize that I could still see the head of a practice torpedo bobbing up and down whilst looking for it through the periscope at a distance of four miles, so it really wasn't that bad! Furthermore, I have never had to wear glasses.

Like all specializations the Submarine Service had its own traditions and oddities. At sea we were genuine pirates wearing a variety of togs such as aertex shirts and old grey flannels. The submarine sweater although white when issued became a dirty shade of grey and became a treasured possession. The food was supplemented by what were called 'Submarine Comforts'. These were considered to be luxury items, although nowadays I do not think that the word would apply. The 'Comforts' consisted of things like tinned fruit and tinned steak and kidney pudding. Submariners had their own glossary for many of these foods. Tinned tomatoes were 'train smash', the steak puddings were 'babies' heads', herrings in tomato sauce -'HITS' or 'herrings in', tinned sausages – 'snorkers' or 'soya links' (they were particularly foul!). The food at sea then was not at all great and it would be difficult for someone brought up in today's Navy to appreciate how low a standard we endured as there was no choice, only one chef and a ridiculously small galley and very limited refrigeration.

CHAPTER 5

Submarines HMS *Sturdy* and HMS *Trump*, Malta

1951–52: HMS *Sturdy*

M Y FIRST REAL APPOINTMENT AFTER completion of Submarine Training was to HMS *Sturdy* in the Mediterranean. She was exactly the same configuration as a World War II 'S class' boat. She had no periscopic radar, no snort and still had a 3-inch gun. I was to be the Navigating Officer. Malta was fine for fixing visually in the submarine operating areas, as there were so many churches. The only problem was identifying them.

Sturdy had no automatic plotting table so everything had to be by hand plotting and estimation. The log was not very reliable and on occasions the gyro did not seem too accurate either. All this led to me making one monumental navigational error, when due to the currents as well, I was 18 miles out of position!

I started off with Jo Perowne as Captain and he was relieved by Peter Samborne. This was his first Command and he was junior boy in the squadron. Many of the COs were ex-wartime and much decorated. One of them was Donald Cameron VC, and the Captain in charge of the squadron was the famous Crap Miers VC. The Commander SM was Mike Lumby who had been a very distinguished CO in the war. A few years later he was to be my Captain SM when I commanded *Osiris* and also when I became 'Teacher' to the Submarine CO's Course.

In company with the Depot Ship, HMS *Forth*, the squadron toured the Mediterranean in those long gone days. The Squadron was then known as the First Squadron. A visit to Trieste allowed us some leave in Austria at an Officer's rest house, near Klagenfurt, with an attractive 9-hole golf course attached.

I particularly remember the Chief of Police's Alfa Romeo in Trieste. He proudly showed us the engine, all enamel and stainless steel!

I acquired the taste for Roulette in the casino at Klagenfurt in spite of the longest run in red numbers when I was backing black. A trip to the Venice casino produced three happy nights. Number 29 on the carré was a great success on the last night. The rich Italians and their ladies, who staked more on one spin of the wheel than I got for a month's pay, flinging large square chips all over the table, made a lasting impression.

The battle of St Mark's Square will go down in history in Venice. A lovely fight developed one night between the submariners and the Italian locals. A large shore patrol had to be landed to sort it all out and was headed by the Squadron's Engineer Commander clad in full white uniform with black gaiters.

We also went to Naples but this was immediately prior to our Sea Inspection so I was extremely busy and saw very little of the place. I did go to a ball at the Town Hall and danced with a heavily chaperoned Italian beauty. She spoke no English and I certainly spoke no Italian so it was back to Fractured French, which I had forsaken many years ago in favour of learning Russian!

It was at Naples that I had the unforgettable experience of seeing and hearing the legendary Gracie Fields. She came onboard HMS *Forth*, the squadron depot ship, at lunchtime and gave a concert to the assembled submariners. She had a marvellous voice and with no microphone, amplifiers and music enthralled us all. Her rendition of 'Sorrento' had the Italian dockies joining in from the quayside, such was the power and attraction of this unique entertainer. She was then living in Capri, which was conveniently close to us in Naples.

A French submarine, an ex German Type XI U-boat, visited Malta and secured alongside *Forth*. We hosted them, and I remember going onboard for drinks. We had a drink, then up on the upper deck for a smoke and then down below to repeat the cycle. This was because the German submarine had open-top batteries so smoking below was *verboten*!

Submarine wardrooms frequently invited each other for lunch-time drinks. Once *Sturdy* invited *Sanguine*'s CO and officers over for 'horses necks'. This was now the naval drink of brandy and ginger ale, having replaced the ubiquitous pink gin. The *Sanguines* arrived alongside by boat having borrowed it from somewhere and drove it

HMS Sturdy 1951

themselves. Unfortunately when it came to the point we had no ginger ale or brandy left onboard. This caused the CO of *Sanguine*, Brian Mills, to write in our Visitors' Book '*Où est le gorge de cheval?*' We ditched some 12 different bottles after this party and they had some difficulty with their boat handling on leaving *Sturdy*!

When the Submarine Squadron visited French North Africa we had a rugger match organized against the French Navy in Algiers. When we ran out onto the pitch we saw that it was made entirely of sand, not a blade of grass in sight. Throughout the match Crap Miers (the Captain SM) was furiously shouting for us to 'Go Low' in our tackling. He was expecting us to tackle them in normal rugger fashion! The only chap who went 'Low' in the whole match was a French wing three-quarter who was carried off after scoring his try bleeding like a stuck pig. The French were playing with a small rugby ball and they could throw it from one side of the pitch to the other as it fitted neatly in the hand. This made the Line Outs a bit difficult for us! We lost heavily. We did rather better at hockey though.

I did have a winning streak at the Algiers casino, this time backing odd numbers. It was a very cosy one-Roulette table affair and almost like a private party compared to Venice.

Whilst serving in *Sturdy* I qualified as a Shallow Water Diver. We did our training in Msida Creek, amongst the sewage discharged by the depot ship and the submarines. After diving we had our ears washed out by the simple expedient of bending our head over each way and having a solution of dettol poured into each ear. No Health and Safety regulations then and we survived quite easily! We used a Salvus set breathing oxygen and wore a rather cumbersome suit. The diving depth was limited to about 30 feet (two atmospheres, the limit for breathing oxygen under pressure). In March, one day I was diving on *Sturdy's* propellers in order to file off any burrs. I dived in swimming trunks as it was a bit of a bore to don a suit. I have never been so cold in all my life sitting on the casing waiting for the next dive and was red with cold all over!

Peter Samborne introduced us to the Time Bearing Plot to help solve the 'Bearings Only' problem posed by purely passive sonar information. As Navigator I was coping with three things at once, a hand-plotted ship's track as we had no plotting table, drawing bearing lines filtered from the time bearing plot and a relative velocity plot where one selected three different speeds and another type of plot which I cannot really remember. He was a brilliant 'attacker' and it was easy to see why he went on to be the Officer in Charge of the Rothesay Attack Teacher and to do so much in introducing the new Torpedo Control System (TCSS3) into service. Later on he was the first Captain of *Dreadnought* and was top of his class whilst doing the American Nuclear Course which converted people into Nuclear Engineers. It was said that as a First Lieutenant he took a 267PW radar to pieces onboard his submarine and mended it. I could well believe that.

I left *Sturdy* after doing a short period as Torpedo Officer, which also meant being Gunnery Officer. We won the Captain SM's shoot, which was a very important affair judged from surfacing until ten rounds had been fired against the clock. Time versus accuracy was very important. Pete Samborne took over the spotting corrections before I could ruin things and *Sturdy* won easily!

So waving goodbye to *Sturdy* homeward bound to the UK I went to *Trump* as the Torpedo Officer, called the Third Hand in those days, with added responsibility for Secretarial matters loosely called Correspondence, the gun, pyrotechnics and sonar. I had had a very good grounding in submarining in *Sturdy* and was very thankful for this happy introduction to the boats.

I purchased my first car during this time. It was a new green Morris Minor, bought on hire purchase. It was a pleasure to drive and I learnt to drive quickly and gained my Maltese driving licence after just a few lessons. My brother gave financial assistance to complete the purchase before I left Malta and eventually imported into the UK.

There are two comical memories of Lord Louis Mountbatten, then the Commander in Chief of the Mediterranean Fleet. He visited *Sturdy* and proudly showed us his white plastic cap cover, it being the only one of its kind then. He had a rather hostile audience as we ruined our cotton ones daily with oil, grease and rust from our little old submarine. The Fleet visited Toulon and Lord Louis ordered that we should adopt some odd rig of reefer jacket but long white trousers. The sailors also had some hybrid uniform and were not allowed to walk along the jetty to the Depot Ship unless suitably attired! I had a rather tubby cheerful torpedo rating who said he felt like Gypsy Rosie Lee (a famous stripper then) as he changed his uniform just about every time the bell struck. Once again the rusty and greasy hatches took their toll of our white uniform.

We were all heartily glad to learn that the Fleet fired its 21-gun salute an hour too early when visiting Algiers as they got the time zone wrong, much to Lord Louis's dismay, as he was such a man for protocol!

1952: HMS *Trump*

I have a photograph of a resplendent torpedo space of *Trump*, which we painted during an Easter weekend. It never looked so smart again! A trip to Gibraltar saw most of the Squadron's officers off to Jerez in a coach by kind invitation of Saccone and Speed – the Company that supplied most of the Royal Navy's wardrooms with their bar requirements in those days. At Jerez we had a splendid lunch preceded by sampling the Williams and Humberts sherries, of which there was a bottle of each variety on each table at which sat four of us. I particularly liked a sherry called 'As you like it' then; it is not available nowadays. I had no trouble in polishing off most of the bottle before turning my attention to Walnut Brown. Lunch was delicious but a bit of a blur but I do remember a fascinating visit to the Bodega.

HMS Trump *1952*

They Who Dare, *filming with Dirk Bogarde*

Trump was involved in a film called *They Who Dare*. It starred Dirk Bogarde among others. I was the film liaison officer and was positioned on the raft whilst they filmed the diving and surfacing shots. I also acted as a Greek Officer pacing up and down the casing in Malta Dockyard whilst the commandos' equipment was being loaded for the oncoming 'raid' against an 'Axis' airfield. Lewis Milestone was the Director. He had directed that masterpiece *All Quiet on the Western Front* of yesteryear. No one would pretend that this film was a masterpiece! Although we sat through it several times just to see the wonderful acting of that Greek Officer!

By being involved with the Film Company I got some memorable photos of *Trump*, particularly internal shots, for my albums. Later I went to the First Night in London and also had lunch with Harold Siddons, who took the part of the Greek Submarine's Captain's Naval advisor, at his club in London. For some unknown reason he committed suicide much later. Akim Tamaroff was also starring in the film and I remember him as quite a character.

Trump was at anchor in Syracuse harbour when we received a signal 'The King is Dead'. This had some interesting repercussions as it meant the Squadron going home for the Coronation Fleet Review and *Trump* being left behind in Malta as she was scheduled to go to South Africa to work with the South African Navy.

The submarine went to Durban via the Suez Canal, Aden and Mombasa. Aden was to be remembered for meeting up with the American who kept his gin in the fridge and just showed the cork of the martini bottle to his ice-cold gin when producing delicious martinis. I had my wallet stolen by a pickpocket in Aden while taking a boat trip back to *Trump*. I have been suspicious of people being pickpockets ever since.

Mombasa was then really quite unspoilt and Kenya was in the midst of the Mau Mau trouble. Max Bacon (our Navigator) and I stayed with the Shell rep, who lived a wonderful bachelor existence in a luxurious house with servants. He had just come back from fighting the Mau Mau and had some horrific stories to tell. He liked his liquor so we were very well looked after.

On to Durban. I remember getting tired of being soaked by the passage through the waves of the Indian Ocean whilst watchkeeping on the bridge, so I tried for just one watch only clad in swimming trunks. I did not repeat this experiment as I was frozen just after 30 minutes. Seawater may be warm there but being continually deluged makes one very cold!

Durban was a wonderful place to see in 1953. Natal was not deeply involved in Apartheid although I remember, on my last night, talking to my taxi driver as he drove round from Durban to the Naval Base on the other side of the water. We got deeply involved in considering the Apartheid problem. I recall him saying that all the Police and Civil Service with an English background were being shipped off to the Boer states and being replaced by Afrikaners. It was a pity that Natal could not see its way clear to secede from the Union and remain British!

The South African Navy at that time was largely officered by ex Brits. You could not be promoted beyond the rank of Lieutenant until you had passed an Afrikaans examination. In the washroom a very senior Lieutenant with last war medals used to greet me with 'Sir'. I was then a very junior Lieutenant and he said I would be a Lieutenant Commander well before him, hence the 'Sir'.

The film of the Coronation was flown out to Durban so I showed it to myself in the wardroom of *Trump* when I was duty one night. I offered the chance to see it to the duty watch but they were just not interested!

Submarines in the Med squadron were then painted 'Mediterranean Blue'. This was an expensive paint but did look very appealing! It was the done thing for the Second Coxswain, a Leading Seaman in charge of the upper deck, ropes etc, to pinch as much as he could from neighbouring submarines so as to avoid having to expend our meagre allowances. At weekends it was customary to oil over the paintwork with shale oil to give the blue paint a nice shine. In harbour all the upperdeck brass fittings were rigorously polished, as were the gun dials etc. We were anything but warlike in those days. I remember one clear day when dived off Malta at periscope depth being able to read the brass nameplate on the gun from the periscope. The Mediterranean was often so clear that an aircraft could track a submarine at about 100 feet visually and certainly on such occasions you could clearly see the bottom of the cliffs at Gozo going quite deep down.

HMS Trump, *return to UK 1953*

Trump returned to England in November 1953 and my parents met her on arrival at Fort Blockhouse. By now we had a new Captain, John Varley, a DSC from World War II. We only did a few trips from Gosport to the areas south of the Isle of Wight before I left for leave and my next appointment. I clearly remember the Captain saying to Hugh Begg, a young Sub Lieutenant, who had joined us to gain experience and was navigating the submarine, 'They don't teach you young buggers to navigate these days', as he banged the parallel rulers onto the face of the plotting table on which the chart rested. The glass cracked, only for him to say 'Now look what you have made me do'.

It was through Hugh Begg, who had joined as a supernumerary, that I met my future wife on a blind date – in November 1953. We were officially engaged on 21 May 1954, her birthday. Hugh resigned from the RN soon after we were married. He then had a remarkably successful career in the publishing business starting off in Kemsley Newspapers and soon became the managing director of Thompson Television (International). He used to say that he then travelled more miles by air than a BOAC pilot! He was the founding father of *Yellow Pages* and several years later was concerned with their introduction in the Eastern Bloc. Unfortunately the punishing pace at which he worked over all the years took its toll and he died at the age of 65 from an aneurysm, having already had open-heart surgery in middle age. Hugh's mother was very much a Fairy Godmother to Tricia and me and certainly made a major contribution to our romance!

I learnt a lot from *Trump*, particularly about how to be a First Lieutenant and how to be the Boss! I believe the lessons stood me in good stead in the years ahead. You may as well learn from other people's mistakes as well as your own. I am sure that those who served under me did likewise!

CHAPTER 6

First Lieutenant HMS *Trespasser* and HMS *Thermopylae*

1954: HMS *Trespasser*

I WAS GIVEN WHAT IS KNOWN AS A 'pier head jump' to join *Trespasser*. She belonged to the 5th Squadron based at Gosport. I had been in HMS *Alliance* gaining A boat experience in Derry waters. Charlie Hammer was the Captain and Bosun Greig the First Lieutenant. I had a lot of fun over the few days that I was onboard. It was a very happy submarine. On arrival back from sea at Londonderry I was instructed to join *Trespasser* at Dartmouth! I flew to Yeovilton in the back seat of a Firefly with my gear in a grip on my knees, from there by train and ferry to Dartmouth.

My turnover from Gervis Frere-Cook was not very valuable nor detailed! On the first dive I had cause to order 'A' Kingston valve to be opened in order to get more water in this forr'd tank to trim the submarine. The 'Outside ERA', who manned the panel at Diving Stations did not know how to operate the lock on the handle! This was not exactly inspiring and indicative of how submarines were operating in those days. There was no planned maintenance then and much relied on the ability and interest of the Engineers.

The Gosport squadron comprised of a mix of submarines then and a 'Reserve Group' of some 3 submarines, which theoretically could put to sea with the Spare Crew. This was really a recipe for disaster and we were lucky not to have a calamity. Apart from exercises the Squadron did a lot of running for the submarine training classes undergoing instruction at the Submarine School at Fort Blockhouse in Gosport. One activity was the so-called three-day cruise, actually two and a half days, as we sailed on Monday morning and got back on Wednesday afternoon. As First Lieutenant I spent hours and hours in the Control Room, as my Captain did not appear to trust anyone else even though the training of the ratings concerned was fairly elementary. Quite often on Fridays we did a half day diving in the very confined and shallow area just south of Lee on Solent. Here I spent a lovely time at periscope depth getting young stokers to operate their ballast pumps and six valve chests pumping and flooding to orders from the Control Room, usually with everything else fully shut off so no harm could be done by their activities. Once again I had to be in the Control Room throughout. This routine did not interfere very much with my courting activity although going up to London after a three-day cruise, with not a lot of sleep, and coming back in the early hours, perhaps to sail at 8 a.m., was a good test of ardour and youth as well as my Morris Minor.

We had a good trip to Oporto in Portugal where I bought some furniture, a reproduction escritoire and a small chest of drawers. They were all stowed in the Torpedo Compartment without damage and made the voyage home safely. Both of these items now have pride of place in our sitting room today as a constant reminder of those far off days. In Oporto I acquired a taste for Grahams' Port, as we were looked after by their manager there.

I think I have fallen down most of the openings in submarines by not looking where I was going. One very painful experience was in *Trespasser* just before going to Harbour Stations prior to entering Portsmouth harbour. The Captain poked his head into the wardroom and asked me to come to his cabin I leapt up and followed him. Unfortunately for me the magazine hatch just outside the wardroom was open and I walked into thin air leaving one leg behind. I do not recommend this trick!

One exercise is indelibly printed in the history of *Trespasser*. It was called 'Bright Bonfire Nine'. It took place in November in the North West Approaches. It was replacement exercise for what had been known as Flag Officer Submarine's summer war. The submarines were to behave as World War II boats making long passages on the surface zigzagging vigorously in very heavy seas acting as a target for other submarines. We also spent periods at 250 feet, I cannot remember exactly why but it must have been a safety requirement for depth separation. *Trespasser* was getting old. We were down to only one workable ballast pump. At 250 feet she leaked like a sieve and we had to come to periscope depth after a

HMS Trespasser *1954*

maximum of two and a half hours as the motor room bilges just filled with water. The ballast pump could not cope with pumping out at that depth and we had to come up shallow with a very small bow-up angle to avoid flooding the motors. As this was conducted at Diving Stations and eventually took one and a half hours with only me allowed on the Trim, this proved to be a tiring exercise as we were also keeping watch one in three.

The Captain, Leo Temple Richards, was quite relaxed in harbour but when we were at sea he became a completely different person. I am sure that we could have easily stopped zigzagging in heavy seas. *Trespasser* was stored for war for the exercise. This meant that the Accommodation Space and passage had a false deck of boxes to provide the space for six weeks supply of canned food plus two weeks emergency supplies, as we could not accommodate all this in the dry provision store. The Torpedo Officer fell out of his bunk one day and smashed the wardroom table. We spent the rest of the exercise perched on baked bean boxes etc at meal times. Crockery breakage was also a problem and by the end the Wardroom was down to single figures in cups – just one!

When we surfaced to charge the batteries, I do not believe we snorted because of the safety rules we were working, the first thing was to 'change lock on the gun' (remember we were acting World War II!). One night the Steward opened the lower lid to the gun tower, which was partially flooded, as the upper lid had leaked. If you can imagine the wall of water coming down and drenching him solely illuminated by the red lighting! It was and remains one of the funniest things I have ever seen. We all ended up in fits of laughter. Fortunately the Captain was on the bridge. He would not have seen the joke at such a serious time as surfacing in a wartime scenario! Since our battery boards were not at all watertight you could see the sparks below as the sea mixed with amps.

We paused at the end of Bright Bonfire Nine and anchored in Loch Eriboll, which is right at the top west corner of Scotland. A hurricane blew up and we were forced to use the motors to take the strain off the anchor cable for about an hour and a half. Our elephant's trunk and bird bath – both made of canvas and used to capture seawater coming down the conning tower in bad weather – had been drying out on the jumping wire. The wind tore them loose never to be seen again so eventually we had to fashion a makeshift arrangement out of odd bits of canvas for the passage home. This was the first and only occasion that I have seen a waterfall going backwards!

On return to Gosport *Trespasser* was declared non-operational. The casing was a wreck and the supports of one of the after facing external torpedo tubes had been torn away by the rough seas. She now leaked like a sieve with no real suction on both of the ballast pumps. I learnt a lot in *Trespasser* including the fact that the Engineer Officer and the Electrical Officer used to pinch my cigarettes as I used to leave them on the shelf by my bunk. I realize that, in retrospect, I had a very tolerant Ship's Company to deal with! They kept their sense of humour in very trying conditions.

Christmas was approaching and so was my wedding, my thoughts were now for the future and taking up my new appointment as First Lieutenant of *Thermopylae*, a newly converted T boat refitting in Chatham. Therefore, I was not particularly sad to say farewell to the dear old *Trespasser*. I got a good report from the Captain, which was nice, as he was a bit of a stickler!

November 1954 to February 1956: First Lieutenant HMS *Thermopylae*

Thermop as she was known was nearing completion of a long refit at Chatham, being converted from a basic T class submarine to a T conversion. Chatham Dockyard had become the expert dockyard for this work. *Tiptoe* was all but complete when I arrived so I could learn a lot from them. In those days Chatham was the best refitting yard. All the trades were good and the management was dedicated to submarines and their safety.

The First Lieutenant of a refitting submarine actually has a lot on his plate! He is responsible for organizing the stores, watchbill and ship's orders as well as such things as cupboards, furniture and painting etc. He also has to fit in with the requirements of the two Technical Officers – the Marine Engineering Officer and the Electrical Officer. As there were now four battery sections and different motors as well as more modern equipment the electrical task merited a dedicated officer. Furthermore *Thermopylae* was to be the trials platform for the new Type 187 sonar. The array was mounted under an expensive stainless steel dome on the casing at the bow.

The Captain was David Scott, who later became an Admiral, first as CBNS Washington and then as Chief of the Polaris Executive. He was to be the Captain of HMS *Surprise*, the Commander in Chief Mediterranean's yacht, as a Commander, and I met up with him then when I was CO of *Talent*. He also drove HMS *Fife* as a Captain. One way and another our paths crossed frequently but he never did remember that when he was Flag Lieutenant to C-in-C Pacific Fleet when I was Midshipman of the Watch, he arrived on *London's* quarter deck and demanded to know where the Admiral's barge was. I simply pointed to the boom where the barge was neatly tied up. He had forgotten to tell anyone that the Admiral's barge was required at this time to take him ashore! Panic stations!

At the beginning of January Tricia and I were married at St Mary the Boltons in London. There was a strong naval presence including my Coxswain and Second Coxswain! Sandy Denleigh-Maxwell, the Chaplain in *London* when I was a Midshipman, officiated. We were

Author's wedding, St Mary the Boltons, 1955

very nervous and so was he. One hymn was missed out completely! After a brief honeymoon in the New Forest we started married life in the wing of a country house in Bapchild near Sittingbourne. It was grand but very cold and Tricia used to dress and undress in the airing cupboard. That winter was extremely cold with snow and ice formed on the inside of the windows. After this start we had to come down with a bump and selected a caravan at the Ideal Home Exhibition that March at Earls Court. This caravan was eventually sited on a farm in the village of Osmington in Dorset. David Scott rented a cottage there called the 'Beehive'.

Thermopylae's workup was pretty basic, as we were to be a trials ship with the new sonar. Consequently we spent many boring days working for the then Underwater Detection Establishment at Portland. We were based at Portland as a member of the 2nd Submarine Squadron with HMS *Maidstone* as the depot ship. All Admiralty scientists were then known as boffins. They had single-track minds. We were taking visual target bearings to one eighth of a degree accuracy (or so they thought). I do not believe that 187 Sonar ever achieved this wonderful bearing accuracy.

When leaving Portland one morning bound for Kiel there was an explosion and a burst of smoke with bits of debris could be seen on the other side of the Depot Ship. This was the *Sidon* affair when an HTP fuelled torpedo blew up killing quite a few people in the Torpedo Compartment and sinking the submarine, albeit alongside. It was not clear to us what had happened until we were well on our way to Kiel. When asked what the purpose of the steel dome covering the Type 187 sonar array actually was a member of the casing party told the German questioner that it was a survival boat that floated on the surface. There were one or two other outrageous suggestions as to its purpose provided by our crew. The passage through the Kiel Canal was fascinating. Although the Germans were then denied Armed Forces there were a mass of different uniforms to be seen. Obviously they loved being in uniforms! I cannot remember much about the visit, which coincided with Kiel Week. We did not see much of David Scott!

During our visit the Flag Officer Rhine, Admiral Campbell Water, and his daughter Fiona, then a famous model, came onboard and we entertained them in the wardroom. I thought she had a rather spotty complexion but then the camera never lies!

One day at Portland when we were waiting to cast off from the jetty after the Captain (F) (the senior Officer of a Frigate Squadron) on the other side had sailed, the said Four Striped Gunnery Lieutenant, as my Captain would say, was bellowing, as Gunnery Officers are prone to do. David Scott was making quite loud remarks about Gunnery Officers in general from our bridge which was not all that far from the bridge of the departing frigate. I just hoped that the aforesaid four-striper did not hear. I must confess that I did share a similar dislike of gunnery officers. As an amateur historian I cannot forgive the Gunnery Branch for not acknowledging the influence of air power on the naval scene nor indeed the submarine threat. They were so engrossed in battleships and big guns that this country was ill prepared for the type of modern warfare experienced in the early days of World War II.

We had one long period away from the UK when we went to the Med for further trials with a lengthy period off Sicily sailing from Syracuse. Syracuse was a fascinating place steeped in history. I must confess I was rather anti a lot of these trials. The boffins had a lovely well-paid existence living ashore in comparative luxury whilst we sweated it out in a rather more primitive environment – such is life!

On arrival in Malta for the first stop there the Officers were invited to have a drink with Jacky Slaughter, the renowned Captain of the Squadron, in his cabin onboard the Depot Ship, HMS *Forth*. He asked us what we would like to drink and the replies varied from gin and tonic to horse's neck with various other tipples in between. Jacky said 'Crowd of f★★★ing teaplanters, get your own!'

I have to record that during my submarine career I was a little 'accident-prone'. I have fallen down most holes or come into contact with most obstructions during my time. I was later amused to read a report written by a 'Work Study' expert who spent a time in the late 1950s onboard a submarine. He lived in the Stokers' Mess during his time onboard a T class submarine and wrote 'You duck to avoid the obvious only to come into contact with the less obvious!' On my first day aboard *Alderney*, with my ankle recently out of plaster and still wrapped in elastoplast, I stepped backwards into one of the holes in the casing and was left floundering holding on to the guardrail and somewhat in pain! I did the same in *Thermopylae* whilst at Malta and drove a piece of my tropical stocking into my shin. This resulted in a stay in Bighi hospital as I also had a bout of 'tropical ear' at the same time. I can remember that I was having sodium nitrite wicks in my ears at the same time as a similar treatment was applied to my shin, such was naval medicine then!

HMS Thermopylae, Malta 1955

We returned to Portland from the Med after 12 weeks away, only for Tricia to find that I had to stay onboard as Duty Officer because of a foul weather warning. This required a qualified 'Driver' to be onboard. I was actually required, as we had to move to secure to a buoy later that day.

A visit to West India Dock by *Thermopylae* later on was quite an experience. The smell cannot be forgotten, as David Scott remarked he had sailed on the Mediterranean Sea and the Red Sea but never the WC! I also remember one night as I approached the Docks entrance a voice from the darkness greeted me by name, Lieutenant Fry. It was a Leading Electrical Mechanic, who had served with me in *Trespasser*, and now a Docks policeman! I handed over as First Lieutenant as we left the Docks in February 1956 and my relief was somewhat surprised to see that I was entrusted with taking the boat out to the river and beyond without the Captain appearing on the bridge.

I had a very happy time in *Thermop*, as she was affectionately known. It was tremendous fun and being newly married and living in a caravan in a lovely rural setting was an idyllic existence. So I left the first submarine to be equipped with TV, the aerial being a piece of wire attached to broomsticks. She was now painted black, as all submarines became black towards the end of 1955. Once again there was a splendid Ship's Company to support me.

CHAPTER 7

First Lieutenant Rothesay Attack Teacher and COs' Qualifying Course

February 1956 to November 1957: Rothesay Attack Teacher

To BE FIRST LIEUTENANT OF THE Rothesay Attack Teacher (RAT) was rightly regarded as a plum job. I relieved Peter Herbert, later an Admiral, who had done a lot of work on the so called Ettrick method. This was a complex mathematical way of solving the bearings only problem faced by a submarine detecting an unseen target. A lot of ideas were being investigated at that time before the advent of computer assistance.

We moved our caravan up to Bute and were lucky to find a site on Bogany Farm as the Duke of Bute would not allow caravans on his land. Farmer Bodys made us very welcome on his farm and we had a marvellous position with wonderful views towards Arran with Loch Ascog in the foreground and towards Largs across the Clyde to the east. The arrival of our son, David, in 1957 saw the purchase of the 'west wing', a smaller caravan with French windows, which allowed the pram to be put under cover in inclement weather. The 3rd Submarine Squadron was then based at Rothesay with its Depot Ship, HMS *Adamant*. Later on the Squadron moved to Faslane which was to become a major submarine base for our nuclear submarines including the Polaris ones.

Although the Attack Teacher had done a lot to advance the new Torpedo Control System, TCSS3, into service the old and tried manual system called 'the Fruit Machine' still existed. An adjunct had been fitted to make it the TCSS2* so that torpedoes could be angled rather than running straight using settings from the machine. The drill was horrendous and would have been so prone to error as to limit its use in war. Setting the torpedoes to run straight as in World War II would have been safer and wiser.

The Officer in Charge of the RAT during my time was Chin Roe. He was a large heavily jowled bachelor. I suspect that he was rather shy but he often gave the impression of being a rather unhappy individual. We got along OK although I cannot say that he contributed much to making life enjoyable at the RAT. With nowhere to go home to he kept long hours and I had to drive him back to his hotel in Rothesay and often had to have a drink at the bar there when I was dying to go home!

I learnt a tremendous amount about torpedo tactics, their weaknesses and the need for better equipment in order to solve the attack problem. I suppose that the main thing I learnt was the importance of bearing rate. If it is steady the target is either a long way off or will collide with you. If it moves fast the target is either very close or very fast! You can appreciate bearing movement when driving a car and waiting to drive out onto a busy road. I learnt that the visual attack is really dead easy when compared to the blind/long range attack or approach which can take hours now that sonar ranges had increased dramatically. The visual attack is over in a matter of minutes rather than hours and you should know what is going on as you can see the target. If only sonar information is available then it is meticulous detective work and patience that are required.

One of my tasks was to draw out the torpedo spread for an angled attack from the data recorded at the end of an attack in the Attack Teacher and to present it as soon as possible for Chin Roe to discuss the results with the team doing the attack. I became very swift and adept at torpedo analysis, which helped me considerably later on. As First Lieutenant I was responsible for the cleanliness and general administration of the RAT. I had a very enjoyable time organizing the repainting of the entire place with less dull and drab service colours with the help of my willing small staff of ratings. I am not sure that Chin Roe appreciated all the colours but the Ship's Company entered into the spirit and the whole place ended up looking very smart. I was most pleased with the dignified black and white scheme of the outside appearance of this old building.

The Attack Teacher had been fitted out by a firm that had normally done stage lighting many years previously. Two targets could be projected on the circular walls by illuminating metal ship models with very powerful lights. This meant that a rather ghostly image appeared for the periscope to observe and take ranges and

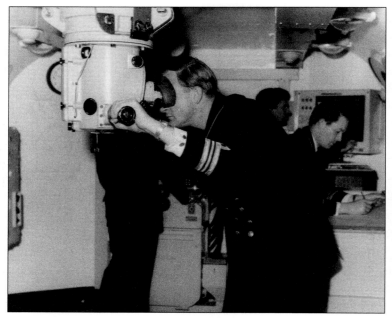

Rothesay Attack Teacher

bearings from. The mini submarine control room revolved inside the cyclorama provided by the walled structure containing it and access to the control room could only be obtained when it had been returned to the start position opposite to the entrance. The control room still had a conning tower and lids so that surface attacks could have been simulated in the last war. In the outbuildings were the remains of an old Attack Teacher of pre-war vintage, which was later used as a pigsty. The whole place was a piece of submarine history and many years later I went to the wake and it was then demolished. It was very strange to see a green field site there many years later.

Caravan life on Bogany Farm was idyllic. The farm had two heavy farm horses that used to put their large heads over the barbed wire of our little compound complete with its small garden. One night a hurricane blew through western Scotland and very high wind speeds were recorded. It blew over our smaller caravan and even the big one was feeling the strain.

The American nuclear submarine, *Nautilus*, called in at Rothesay. As it was the very first of its type in the world it had a hand picked

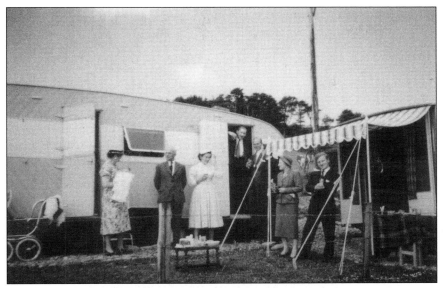

Caravan Home, Bute 1957

team of officers. There was a splendid party to welcome them and they were happily consuming large quantities of whisky. My wife said to one of them 'I suppose that you're the cream of the submarine service?' To which came the reply 'We like to think so Ma'am'. There was a very strong poker school amongst the younger officers led by the Doctor whose rapid rise in rank because of his profession was the envy of junior officers of similar age and produced much chaffing!

Like all good things my time at the RAT came to an end. It was super to be home every night and when the Depot Ship left Rothesay Bay to transfer the squadron to Faslane we became the sole naval presence in the Isle of Bute. I suppose I stayed too long at the RAT and was a bit divorced from the sea when I started my COs' course. We sold the caravans and had a fistful of Scottish £5 notes thrust upon us at Glasgow Central Station in payment for the small one on the night we left for London and Christmas. We were very trusting to agree to this method of payment and had not realized that English banks could be chary of Scottish banknotes!

It was sad to say goodbye to caravan life. We had lots of people to stay as well as to have a meal with us. Our son's Christening was a splendid affair with the red and white awning attached to the small caravan and a lovely blue sky to enhance the champagne reception chez nous.

1957–58: COQC

My COs' qualifying course is really something I do not remember much about. I suppose this was because it was a busy time. Rud Cairns was my 'Teacher' and as reference to his obituary in the Submarine Museum's yearbook reveals, a highly respected one too. He was very relaxed.

We did our seagoing weeks in HMS *Talent* and our main target in those days was HMS *Blackwood*, a Type 14 Frigate. We had an instant problem as the Attack Periscope in a T class submarine had no 'high power' magnification. All we could see to range on and make angle on the bow estimations was the normal image that the naked eye would see. As *Blackwood* was a small ship in any case it proved difficult to get good ranges. Determining her course by estimation of angle on the bow was also a little more difficult. It certainly made you thankful for high power on the more modern attack periscopes later in life. Still, I suppose this drawback was good for us.

We had the usual time in the Attack Teacher at HMS *Dolphin* and at the Rothesay Attack Teacher. The target presentation was much better at *Dolphin* as the ship models were visual and not projected. They were somewhat difficult to take seriously as they appear to fly since they were suspended from a moving contraption.

The visit to Barr and Stroud at Glasgow was very enjoyable and was a delight to see a firm that practised good old fashioned engineering. Their periscopes were the best in the world thanks to the splendid optics. In those days lenses were produced and polished entirely by hand.

We went ashore at night putting up in the Victoria Hotel in Rothesay while the submarine secured to a buoy in the harbour. As it was a winter course the early morning starts were cold, often wet and very bleak. I cannot remember much about the actual content of the course except to remember the countless attacks in the Attack Teacher at HMS *Dolphin* at Gosport. 'Blind Attacks' at sea, when the attack relied on sonar information only, were over so quickly because of the short sonar detection ranges. The word 'Blind' was a really good description and we often had little or no idea of where the target was.

So, thankfully I passed and went on leave to await my First Command appointment. Having wracked my brains to write some more about this important event in a submariner's life I confess to having been defeated by the passage of time!

CHAPTER 8

First command HMS *Acheron*

April 1958 to April 1959

AFTER MY COS' COURSE I WAS initially earmarked for HMS
Scotsman, a converted S class submarine with an extra battery
and capable of fairly high speeds. She was carrying out trials for
future submarine design and conducting lots of high-speed
experiments. Luck shone on me yet again and I had a hurried
telephone call whilst on leave instructing me to join HMS *Acheron*
at Faslane. As far as I can remember I arrived the night before we
sailed. My turnover from the departing CO consisted of being given
the spare set of Confidential Book safe keys on the jetty before I
boarded the submarine, already at Harbour Stations, and prepared
to sail for the first day of workup!

I did not know any of the Officers. However, I did have a
splendid team. Dick Horner was the First Lieutenant, Tom Green
as the Navigator, Tony Harris was the Torpedo Officer and Vic
Gunson was the Engineer. Sadly Dick Horner was killed in a car
accident several years later when he was standing by HMS *Valiant*,
then building at Barrow, as her Executive Officer.

The first day of your first submarine command is something
special, yet I did not feel anything particularly significant. I had
trained for this moment for many years and it arrived with no
fanfare. Workup was just what I needed as Captain as I could
determine how the submarine was to continue her commission. I
was very lucky, as I have had the privilege of working up every one
of my submarine commands. On completion of workup *Acheron*
joined the 5th Squadron at Gosport.

The Captain's cabin in an A class submarine is situated in the
small boiler drum-like structure that leads off the conning tower.
When the submarine is dived it really meant that I did not use the
cabin since the lower lid of the conning tower was normally shut
for safety reasons. During exercises my usual sleeping position was

the Captain's chair in the wardroom with my head on the wardroom table. I remember after one Londonderry exercise being virtually out for the count and they had some difficulty in waking me!

I cannot say that the A class was my favourite class of submarine. They did have some attractions; the sewage tank was splendid, as you did not have to blow direct to sea after using the 'heads'. The battery sections were more accessible than those of the T class and did not have battery boards. I do not think that the diesel engines were so reliable as those were in T boats. The ability to fire torpedoes from the stern as well as the bow was a distinct plus.

Navigation remained primitive to say the least. Poor navigation was responsible for me hitting the bottom when we dived one night to escape air attack and went to 150 ft only to hit a large bank that rose to 135 ft. My poor First Lieutenant had had to make do with one Loran line among other things and the wonderful world of surface navigators said a lot of rude thing about our navigation after the Board of Inquiry. They were not there on a pitch-black night in a roughish sea making a so-called passage against air opposition in an area with little or no navigational aids. The staff at Londonderry had decided to give Coastal Command a chance so we were not allowed to snort and had to do a surface passage and escape attack as best we could! Navigation in those days off Malin Head in winter was never an exact science. Out of the blue, an Officer who had been riding with us wrote from New Zealand some 45 years later recollecting this little incident!

The exciting thing about being based at Gosport was the tide in Portsmouth harbour. A submarine backing out of Blockhouse Creek just hoped to turn towards seaward before the ebb tide carried it beam on. One day we never made it and we were swept out of the harbour entrance sideways, much to the astonishment of the American Captain who was serving on the Staff and was with us that day. He had to go to sea periodically to continue to receive submarine pay!

Coming into harbour was also somewhat difficult, particularly at night. There was a chart of times that you were allowed to enter depending on the times of High and Low water. There was a theoretical period called the 10-minute stand when the ebb tide was

HMS Acheron, *Author's first Submarine Command, at Londonderry 1958*

slack and theoretically it was safe to come in. The dodge was to go up harbour and wait until the theoretical happening occurred. It was easier in daylight as one could see the effect of the tide on buoys etc. One night we came perilously close to 'Promotion point' as it was called because the tide caught us as we turned to enter Haslar Creek. I could clearly see the bottom and backed out as fast as I could. No harm done but a valuable lesson in tidal effects. I remember Henry Cook, who was Captain of HMS *Alaric*, driving her into the jetty at about 10 knots, wiping off the bow dome and giving his casing party a big fright. The resulting mark was known as the *Alaric* mark thereafter.

Acheron did some basic training class running but plenty of exercises both at Portland and Londonderry as well as National and NATO major events. Londonderry, where the Joint Anti-Submarine School was based, always presented a challenge, including the passage up the Foyle. It was recognized that the Irish pilots were somewhat free-range and one of their methods in the upper reaches was to run along the edge of the shadows of the trees! One of them let me speed up to 15 knots when it was actually pretty shallow, as the stern disappeared under water, this being known as shallow water effect, I slowed down. On those occasions when we did not take a pilot I could claim pilotage money and took my First Lieutenant and Navigator out for steak eggs and chips as they always helped with the pilotage. The cost then of a fair sized portion was 4 shillings and 6 pence, 22½p in today's inflated money.

We were entrusted with the submarine training of the Dreadnought's future medical team. There were two doctors, a Chief Petty Officer Sick Berth Attendant and two Petty Officers. The Sick Berth Attendant title eventually became Medical Technician. The picture of the Control Room's main watchkeeping positions manned by this illustrious medical team was a sight for sore eyes and I shudder to think what the Geneva Convention would think about it. They were with us for a month and it was a very enjoyable experience and I hope that their experience in *Acheron* proved to be valuable to them later on.

Our only home visit was to Swansea, which was great fun. I gather that the mayor collected his dole in the mayoral Rolls Royce. I played golf with the harbour master on a quaint golf course near the harbour. One of his chums playing a hole alongside ours but in the opposite way topped his approach shot as we passed. The harbour master said 'Dai, you played that like a gypsy's donkey, all skin and tool'. That is the best description of a topped iron shot that I have heard and I often quote it on the golf course, when playing a customary bad shot.

In these early days after World War II the wartime days were fresh in the memory of senior officers particularly. When the first post-war German submarine 'Shark' visited Fort Blockhouse in Gosport (which was the Alma Mater of the submarine service then) the German captain arrived in the staff office to say farewell to the Captain SM. After the CO had left the Captain SM said that he was glad that he had eczema on both hands, they were heavily bandaged, as he could never have shaken hands with him. No one should ever forget the heavy losses experienced by our submarines during the war, especially in the Med, and the survivors lost a lot of their friends.

So I enjoyed my first Command at the ripe old age of 28. We lived in a new Married Quarter in Gomer Lane in Gosport and there were plenty of submariners on this patch.

My next appointment came as a bit of a surprise. I had been expecting to go to Malta to the Joint Tactical School there. A lovely married-accompanied shore job as the submarine 'expert' on the staff there. What more could a man ask? What indeed! The trouble is that after one's first Command it was then necessary to do two years of 'General Service'. In those days the Chief of Staff to Flag Officer Submarines controlled CO's appointments. He was then a very distinguished CO from World War II, George Hunt. He sent for me and said that he now had in mind for me to go as a Course Officer at *Royal Arthur* – the Petty Officer's Leadership School. 'How does that strike you, Fry,' he asked, 'like a blow between the eyes?' I could but agree and several of my chums laughed a lot when they heard the sad news!

CHAPTER 9

HMS *Royal Arthur* Petty Officers' School

May 1959 to February 1961

ROYAL ARTHUR WAS FAR FROM THE SEA situated at Corsham in Wiltshire. Corsham was a small village and the school was well off the beaten track. Accommodation was not easy to find, and as we were not exactly rich, we settled on renting a schoolmaster's cottage near Lacock. The only problem being that we had to evacuate the cottage during the summer holidays when he and his family used Holly Cottage as a holiday home. It was a very pretty little thatched cottage with roses growing up the front and often admired by passers by. No two floors were on the same level and they sloped dreadfully. It was all very old worldly: never again afterwards did we have any great longing for a pretty cottage, although we did enjoy our time there.

Royal Arthur was a hot house in more ways than one although I did enjoy lecturing; who does not, as it is a great excuse to have an ego trip? It is easy to see why actors like the stage! After a few courses there was inevitability about the likely outcome. Would the course gel, would they be a spirited bunch, and would they excel at the sporting side, particularly the Dog Watch Games?

The object of the course was to teach Petty Officers and Chief Petty Officers about Leadership. At the same time they were encouraged to enlarge their knowledge from the various lectures and develop skills in lecturing themselves. Physical challenges were presented to them in the 'Cliff and Chasm', an Obstacle Course and a trek in the Black Mountains in Wales. The 'Cliff and Chasm' was probably the most dangerous and would not satisfy today's Health and Safety requirements! A very heavy barrel had to be transported over a course, which was designed to use a sheer leg approach to getting the barrel over the Chasm. It then had to be safely transported down the hill and placed on a carriage for a run home on the flat. It was very exhausting for the combatants! The Obstacle

Course also involved getting a barrel round the Course and the Petty Officers had to negotiate a pond in a Tarzan like fashion as they swung across the water to the other side. There was a time penalty for touching the water.

I had one memorable course, Number 657, which broke the Obstacle Course Record. Teams were given an opportunity to have a run to try and break the record in addition to their normal outing on the Obstacle Course. There were many young Engine Room Artificers in this group, they were intelligent, motivated, fit and had the same background. I found the older Petty Officers (who probably thought that they had escaped the physical rigours of *Royal Arthur*) were rather anti the Leadership Course from the word go and did not set much of an example. The Sick Berth ratings were always good. It was often a mistake to have Leading Rates on these courses; they had either passed and were waiting promotion or were just recommended. Some of them would hardly justify their place on the Course.

My fellow Course Officers were a great bunch and it was easy to strike up a lasting friendship. The Captain was Peter Lachlan and he was very keen on outdoor pursuits. He had inaugurated the Black Mountains Trek as part of the 6-week course. I much enjoyed the time in the Black Mountains. Whilst the Petty Officers spent the night out in the open I was always back at base camp that night just in case anything had gone wrong. The Petty Officers set off at dawn on the first day and so did I. Course Officers always had to replace marker poles reported missing. I walked alone with no food except a bar of chocolate, no water bottle, and the map, but initially, no compass. However, on one occasion I took the wrong ridge in the fog and the sun broke through right ahead of me instead of behind. My bump of locality was very much in error!

I could do up to 40 miles in a day walking although much of the homeward trip had to be on the road as it is not a good idea to be on the hills in the dark. I did not obey this one night, and had to descend the shale strewn slope in gathering darkness to get to some habitation to discover exactly where I was in relation to base camp.

Base Camp was a derelict cottage with outbuildings about half a mile directly uphill from Cwmyoy. On arrival by bus we had to transport the food, boxes of compo rations, fuel for the stove, bags of coke and all the other clobber up the hill. In all the trips I did to

Royal Arthur *course, Black Mountains, Wales*

the Black Mountains I never got wet, but did experience the mist freezing in my hair. Once I was so hot that eventually I was driven to descend some 1500 feet to the stream below for some water to quench an aching thirst; not a good idea as once you have succumbed you just continually want some more.

The Petty Officers were in teams of three with one nominated leader. They had to collect points by visiting as many positions as possible during their trek. Positions could be a marker pole or feature. Marker poles were coloured in various ways. At the end of their trek they had to claim their points by debriefing to their Course Officer, so theoretically there could be no cheating! I am sure there was, particularly when some amazing scores were claimed! Nevertheless the time in the Black Mountains gave them an experience they would not normally have encountered as well as a personal challenge.

There was a very friendly farmer who had a farm right next door to the School. He used to make some vicious brews, cider and barley wine. He had an excellent grapevine; and always knew what went on in *Royal Arthur*.

I had 10 courses at *Royal Arthur*. Each Course lasted six weeks and was pretty intensive. It goes without saying that you had to know all the names and as much as possible about the Course members in as short a time as possible. Their first essay about themselves was avidly read that first night by me in bed. It was amazing to me how many had joined the Navy from broken homes, and there were quite a few ex Barnardo's boys in my courses.

The Dog Watch games were great fun. Course Officers and their Chief Petty Officers played against the Petty Officers as staff teams. Deck Hockey was fraught with danger as the rules were completely disregarded. There were no Health and Safety considerations then! Parade Ground Hockey was wonderful; very tiring as you went from end to end continuously with six a side. The Staff Officers played the Staff Chief Petty Officers for half an hour each way on a fallow Wednesday afternoon! There was a full size skittle alley, which was very popular and was quite unlike the pub game played in Wiltshire, where the ball could so easily pass between the skittles.

The Royal Naval chaplain, Bernard Briggs, at *Royal Arthur* must have special mention. He had an ecclesiastical standeasy on Sundays between the customary matins and communion so that those who did not want to stay for communion did not feel left out. He had a knack of reducing things to basics by exhibiting worldly wisdom instead of flannel. For instance there was a session called the Religious Brains Trust where the Petty Officers could ask questions of a team of padres, Bernard Briggs, an RC vicar and a Free Church man with a layman. I sometimes appeared as a layman. Bernard refuted the RC view of birth control by quipping that shoe leather was artificial and left the RC vicar flabbergasted! Bernard baptized our daughter, Claire, who arrived in July of our first year there, and we have kept in touch with his widow for many years. She is still going strong in spite of now being in her late 80s.

All Course Officers had to give certain lectures to every course in addition to those given to their own course. I was the stand-in lecturer for Prisoner of War indoctrination and this was a splendid talk to give, taking two periods, backed by tape recordings. I could only give this when Paddy Sheehan was away in the Black

Mountains! Alan Tupper and I had a double act presentation about convoys and submarine attack. I suppose that after a time we tried to make this more comical than instructional! Alan had a house in the famous chocolate box village of Castle Combe. He had married the daughter of a wealthy Swiss businessman. Their house had all the attributes of having been furnished entirely by Harrods. There were gold taps in the bathroom! We went to a splendid fondue party at their house with some twelve of us seated around the table. The pièce de résistance was obviously the fondue, which consisted of Swiss cheese mixed with Swiss wine. There was a snag! As Alan mixed up the constituents they took on the consistency of Dunlop rubber. The addition of more wine to this unyielding mass did little to improve the situation. By this time Alan was getting a bit cross and many of us were having fits of laughter! Eventually I had to reverse my chair so that I faced away from the table as I was laughing so much it was extremely painful. I have never laughed so much in my life!

We had outside lecturers who gave talks to all the Petty Officers on Course at that time, and some of them were fascinating. I have particular memories of Jack Daniel, a Constructor from Bath, who was eventually the Director General Submarines. I suppose that this period of my naval life was by far the most physically fit! As a submariner I have always preferred the fat and happy as opposed to the lean and keen. I have learnt this from observing that the physically fit require lots of sleep and are very slow to become fully awake. These two attributes are not to be encouraged in submarines.

So ended a shore job, home most nights, lots of interests and plenty of sport; now I was to get my reward after that 'blow between the eyes' by going to the Med to command HMS *Talent*.

CHAPTER 10

HMS *Talent* in command, Mediterranean and Malta

February 1961 to May 1962

MY REWARD, HMS *TALENT* was a T class Streamline submarine then refitting in the Malta Dockyard. Once again I was lucky with my band of Officers. Keith Pitt was the Navigator and Terry Woods the Torpedo Officer. The Med squadron was now only a fraction of that when I was out there in *Sturdy* and *Trump*. HMS *Forth* was no longer the Depot Ship for the submarines and eventually went to Singapore. Our depot ship then was HMS *Narvik*, an old LST, berthed in Msida Creek in much the same position as that previously occupied by *Forth*. We were now the 5th Division and the Squadron at Gosport had become the First, just to confuse everyone!

Malta Dockyard had recently been privatized and it had been sold to Baileys, a Welsh organization that had no experience of dockyards whatsoever as far as I could gather. I seem to remember that they owned a dock in Wales. Fortunately for us and them the old Malta Dockyard hands were still there and we had a good refit.

One of my aims during the refit was to make the Ship's Company a cohesive whole. Many were married and accompanied by their families, whilst there were plenty of bachelors. We had an archaeological exped across the island and visited many prehistoric sites including Tarxien as well as seeing quite a lot of the island including a boat trip to their Blue Grotto. We made an affiliation with the Highland Light Infantry Regiment then serving in Malta with their C Company and played hockey against them. It was all good fun and kept people occupied. When the refit finished the Ship's Company was well established as a 'band of brothers'.

I well remember an American submarine that had limped into Malta with flooded motors after a snorting accident. I called upon their CO when they were berthed in the Dockyard for repairs and listened in astonishment as the American Captain rang up his motor room frequently from his wardroom to get the latest insulation readings and ignoring me completely. There was one gentleman in that submarine. He was called George and came from Georgia, everyone's idea of a real Southern gentleman. He used to come and visit us in the submarine refitting offices in order to get away from his fellow officers! He was a 'Rickover Reject'. He told us about his interview. Admiral Rickover interviewed all prospective nuclear submarine officers. He had knocked on the door and entered after hearing Rickover say 'Come in'. Rickover took one look at him and said 'Get out you big fat slob'. That was his interview. George was indeed 'well built'.

We had quite a good workup and sea inspection; it was Robbie Alexander's last ride in a submarine of the now renamed 5th Submarine Division. Chimp Clayden was the Commander SM. Due to the downgrading Chimp was relieved by a Lieutenant Commander. Hugo Newton took over from Robbie as Captain SM.

When *Talent* visited Livorno some of us went up to Florence by train. It is a lovely city and provided lots of sightseeing. I had my own guide in the Uffizi Gallery for £3 and he showed me the treasures in the short time I had available. I took some of my officers to Pucci's shop and I purchased a blouse, scarf and nylons for Tricia. It was great fun being the only customers and male at that! A trip to Gucci's was not so successful as it was so expensive and we could only gape!

Malta was a place for super parties, many in fancy dress. We played hard and worked reasonably hard too. At a Roman party my wife was dressed as a high born Roman lady whilst I was a dissident Ancient Briton carrying a 'Go Home Romans' sign. Robbie Alexander looked every inch a Caesar and Mrs Alexander, who was quite tall in any case, was a very convincing and impressive Roman Matriarch. At a Red and White party my wife was a Russian princess and I was a Red Russian. So you can see I was always the uncouth and rough half!

I did all my Ship Command exams in my first few months. The objective was to qualify for a surface ship command. I am not sure what good it did me as the magic notation never ever appeared in the Navy List although I had passed in all the subjects! I put this down to the efficiency of General Service as opposed to us submariners! A sporting confrontation always occurred between HMS *Berwick* (Captain F5) and *Talent*. *Berwick* always won as she had the new Type 177 sonar and a very good Torpedo and Anti Submarine (TAS) Officer, Noel Bearne. We became good friends and I wrote a paper describing the Type 177, as we submariners then knew nowt about it. David Dunbar Nasmith, who had been my House Officer at Dartmouth, commanded *Berwick*. In pursuit of knowledge about Gunnery I spent a day at sea in one of the *Daring* class destroyers. In those days they were all commanded by Captains. On this day the ship sailed with the First Lieutenant in charge. When it came to commence firing the First Lieutenant asked about the wind settings being used. The Operations Room reported the direction completely opposite to that being observed on the Bridge! As quick as a flash the First Lieutenant said 'only God can change the wind direction and he isn't onboard today'!

Talent had the much improved hull mounted sonar Type 169. This was never anyway as good as the new Type 187 but a tremendous improvement on *Acheron*'s old 129. We had a demonstration during one exercise when we were in an anti-submarine role and detected something sounding like rattling tin cans. I selected an arbitrary firing solution based on a normal submarine speed and detection range. We then delivered our attack signal via the underwater telephone much to the surprise of an American Nuclear submarine who was actually about 1500 yards away, so our solution was widely out but he got the shock of his life as he thought he was the hunter and had no idea of our presence!

I was lucky enough to go to sea in three Turkish submarines. Two of these were when they were doing a tactical course at the Joint School in Malta at Manoel Island and one who visited Malta later on. *Piriraeis* and *Canakkale* were the first two. The friendship that resulted meant that when I hitched a lift on a NATO flight to Istanbul I was well looked after by the Turks. I will always remember their delight in getting me to be a 'doctor' for an 'injured belly dancer's hip' at the Istanbul Hilton. I had been ushered forward as a doctor to 'cure' the hip of a gorgeous red head with about an 18-inch waist in response to an announcement by the

Author at Istanbul Hilton, rendering first aid!

master of ceremonies! I was provided with a full set of photos showing me caught in the act immediately after the performance signed by the dancer and her partner. I had to confess all this to Tricia on arrival back at Malta, as I knew that certain 'chums' would take some glee in exposing this piece of cabaret.

Later on *Talent* ended up in Izmir after a NATO exercise. There were a number of submarines there berthed stern to the jetty: a Greek, two British, an American and three Turkish. Once again I was well looked after by the Turks as I had my 32nd Birthday during the visit. I went to a nightclub in company with the Turkish Captain who was their version of our Flag Officer Submarines. His aide went on ahead and said a few words to the Manager, which resulted in all the front seats by the cabaret being hurriedly cleared for our party to sit down to watch the cabaret from the front row! Such was the power of the military in Turkey then. The trip to Ephesus was very interesting although the American CO described it all as a pile of rocks; he obviously had no feeling for history!

I learnt a lot of Turkish during my sea trips and it was my boast (although not strictly true) that I could control a submarine in Turkish! One morning whilst at sea, the First Lieutenant in one of them brought me a tumbler full of whisky to my bunk. I insisted on waiting until 10 a.m. before drinking it! Turkish Submarines were meant to be 'dry' like the Americans – they were not! Turkey was not a very rich country and as a guest onboard it could be embarrassing as I was fed steak and they had none. I refrained from comment as I realized the generosity implied. The belly dance laid on by the Turkish Petty Officers one night at sea was super fun. The ordinary Turkish sailors were all conscripts and regarded as peasants by the regulars. During our last night at Izmir I ended up onboard the Turkish submarine *Pirireis* in the early hours of the morning. The Captain showed me his wardrobe, which had been converted into a capacious wine store and jammed with bottles of Turkish wine! The CO was an authority on high quality carpets and at a party Tricia and I gave for him and his officers in Malta we proudly showed him a carpet we had made with the old hook method many years previously. He turned it over and looked at the back and said 'Ah, it is a blanket'. We had not realized that he actually collected old and valuable carpets with hundreds of stitches to the inch.

Once, in the period between exercises at opposite ends of the Med, we gained a day by steaming hard to achieve 24 hours for us to enjoy. We anchored off a Greek island for an unscheduled visit. Having persuaded the Greek fishermen to take us ashore and to return us to the submarine we were set for a party. I regret that many of the crew got very merry on Retsina (horrid stuff and tasted just like turpentine). We almost exhausted the island's food stocks as they were not very well provided with and were relatively very poor.

There can be no argument that service in the Med for a submariner was a very happy experience. One saw a lot of foreign ports; there was plenty of sport in a pleasant climate. The cost of living in Malta was quite low and submariners had the advantage of being accompanied by their families, unlike the ships. We also had the distinct advantage of meeting up with the surface fleet and seeing how they behaved.

Talent had a splendid time trying to outdo HMS *Seadevil* on every possible occasion. *Seadevil* was the junior boat and being the ugly duckling was determined to outdo the rest of us. I always like to think that we had won the battle of one-upmanship by the time we left in spite of Dick Heaslip, then the CO and later to become FOSM, having a great selection of officers including Paddy O'Riordan and Paddy Ryan when they were both very young! We had a memorable rugger match against *Seadevil* on New Year's Day. The smell of alcohol in the scrum was incredible. I am sure *Talent* won! It was the last time I played rugger.

Talent gave me the chance to experiment. We consumed large quantities of bubble decoys, as they were the one defence against sonar detection in good sonar conditions in the Med. It was possible to seduce the attacking sonar to hold onto the contact from the bubbles whilst you stole away. We also perfected the art of going backward; also useful in breaking contact as the wash from the propellers made some camouflage. I may have also developed the ability of controlling the submarine with an evacuated control room (in case of fire etc) although this may have been properly developed later in *Artful*.

Talent had the record for the longest 'Trot fob' in history. 'Trot fob' is the term submariners use for moving the submarine from one position in a trot of submarines to another. We had the honour of going from the port side of Narvik to the starboard and taking some 3 days to achieve it! This all arose from our visit to Benghazi. When we arrived off the shores of Libya we received a signal saying 'hold it' as the Consul thought that the political situation was such that the presence of a British warship could be unsettling. I think he was talking about impending revolution and the king about to be deposed. Perhaps he could have thought about this before we left Malta! After steaming back and forth off the coast the visit was finally cancelled and back to Malta we went. On the night we arrived alongside *Narvik* it was in the midst of a mess dinner and there were cheers, ribald remarks and plenty of laughs for this elongated movement from one side of *Narvik* to the other!

Talent also nearly succeeded in sinking a minesweeper with her after plane guards, these were the steel projections that protruded just below the waterline to prevent the after planes being damaged when going alongside. One morning, as we backed out of Msida Creek past the long line of minesweepers moored to buoys, we had an electrical failure, which meant loss of the broadcast, and failure of the telegraphs amongst other things. Therefore I watched powerless as the stern sailed on into a line of small marker buoys, thence to hit the side of one of the minesweepers, whilst my First Lieutenant bolted down the conning tower and to the motor room to get some headway on to prevent further consternation amongst the sweepers.

Talent made her way homeward after an exercise with the Mediterranean Flotilla via Barcelona where I purchased a toy donkey on wheels for our daughter Claire, which was given the name of Pepe. He was towed across the main drag in Barcelona by a glamorous dancer from the visiting English Ballet Company! I attended my first and last bullfight here. It was a sad experience and I left half way through. There was no glory or spectacle and I will never attend another as it was really rather distasteful.

Talent arrived at Plymouth at about 11 p.m. on a very dark night and we were ordered to berth past the first trot of three boats onto the second trot. I did not think this was very thoughtful for a submarine just joining the Squadron, who had never been to the Depot Ship berth at the north end of the Dockyard before! All went well and Ian Macintosh (the Captain SM) and Spike Park (the Commander SM) welcomed us with a few drinks before bed.

One of the lasting impressions of Malta was a trip to the beach with the family. The amount of stuff that we transported was considerable and required many trips from our Morris Minor Estate car to the water's edge. There was the pushchair and folding chairs, picnic gear, toys, swimming costumes and towels, changes of clothes etc. etc!

CHAPTER 11

HMS *Artful* and Plymouth

November 1962 to September 1963

I HANDED OVER *TALENT* TO Dick Husk very shortly after our arrival in Plymouth and now joined HMS *Artful*, an A class streamline then refitting in Devonport Dockyard. *Artful* had a very good refit, as Devonport was now very skilled at this art. I had the pleasure of the project manager of our refit saying that our sea trials were just like a workup. There is no better way of testing everything and developing a good Ship's Company early on! The Plymouth Squadron was called the 2nd as the Portland Squadron had been discontinued. The Depot ship was HMS *Adamant*.

At *Artful*'s Commissioning party Tricia was talking to a stranger dressed in a sports jacket. She chatted about Hugo Newton's exploits in the spying game when he was the Naval Attaché in Moscow. She was surprised to be told that she shouldn't know about that. The stranger was the Commodore Naval Intelligence! He was visiting Plymouth and I had said he could come along to our party.

I was yet again lucky with my Officers. Mike Hunt was the First Lieutenant and Geoffrey Biggs the Torpedo Officer, who later became an Admiral.

Artful spent a lot of time at sea as in those days we were operating a system of six weeks operational and two weeks in harbour for leave and maintenance. This was the brainchild of the Flag Officer Submarine's staff. I am glad to say that it was not repeated later on as it was tiring and hard on the equipment. All the submarines in the Squadron were inflicted with this mode of operations so we did not see much of each other. In the married quarters it was the done thing to look after the families of those at sea when it was your turn to be in harbour. I remember sweeping the snow away from next door's front during the severe winter of 1963.

Artful had a good workup. She was a very clean submarine, following in *Talent*'s footsteps, as I am rather hot on cleanliness,

Author's wife cutting cake at commissioning of HMS Artful, *1963*

almost manic and regarded by some as over the top! I shall always remember the occasion prior to our harbour inspection when a CPO came along to the wardroom to complain about the Senior rates having to lay out their polished cutlery for the inspection! He chose the wrong moment as he found me and the Officers doing just that with the wardroom cutlery. There we all were, polishing away with the metal polish. It was traditional then that everyone dug in for the work necessary to get the submarine up to a high standard for Harbour Inspections. I shall always remember the example set by Peter Collinson when he was the Electrical Officer of *Thermopylae* polishing the wardroom deck wearing his mess undress minus jacket but with waistcoat.

Artful had a monkey on the ship's crest so what better than to adopt a gibbon in Plymouth Zoo. The Ship's Company paraded in the zoo and I led the march off with George the gibbon in tow on a lead. He was taken back to the boat and promptly bit the Coxswain's hand amongst his other indiscretions!

The running routine experienced during my time in *Artful* was monotonous and I do not remember very much about it all. We did attend the 150th anniversary of the relief of San Sebastian by Wellington. *Artful* headed the line with a Spanish ship and a French destroyer as we passed close offshore as a review part of the celebrations. The Spanish entertained us to a magnificent dinner in a disused old church that evening. During our 'sail past' we unleashed a number of coloured signal grenades, red and yellow, to denote the Spanish flag. I am not sure why they wanted to pay tribute to this particular anniversary since Wellington's troops went on the rampage after taking the city with rape and pillage being the order of the day!

Artful did a series of trials off the Canary Islands with HMS *Brocklesby*. She was the trials ship for the new sonar to be installed in the nuclear submarines then being built. The 2001 sonar, as it was to be called, was so large that *Brocklesby* only had half an array.

One of the pleasures of submarine attacks in peacetime is to give a sharp reminder to the dozey surface ship. The best time for this is the dawn attack! The opponent's sonar operators are switched off and you can be wide-awake with a nice visual target against the lightening sky. We had an expendable torpedo to fire. This was an old Mk 8 that had an inert head and ran just like the real thing but sank at the end of its run. It allowed a periodical amount of realism, as the target ship should hear the torpedo pass underneath. We attacked a destroyer commanded by an old submariner, Ken Vause, off Londonderry one dawn morning with our expendable and although not required to announce this attack with a green grenade we did just for fun. It was usual practice in exercises to indicate torpedo fire with a green grenade so that analysis of attacks could be carried out. The skyline was lit up with a green light some 1500 yards on his bow. We heard later that complete chaos ensued as he had been asleep at the time and got a rude awakening.

One of the parties that the wardroom gave in Plymouth was memorable for two unrelated reasons. The first being that we had the Bishop of Plymouth as a guest and I showed him my cabin tucked away in the fin. I said later that I had never been so close to heaven! At this same party we had invited the local MP, who appeared to be under the impression that the social gathering was paid for by the taxpayer. This politician was soon told the truth. In those days the Officers paid for their entertainment and this even extended to parties in foreign ports. It was much later on that submarines achieved any financial assistance for their excellent work in promoting the Royal Navy when giving entertainment in foreign ports.

There was an excellent restaurant at Modbury called the Exeter Inn. The proprietor was the cook, waiter and everything else. There was just one sitting and limited numbers and menu. The roast duck was a house speciality, and Tricia and I enjoyed our rare visits there. The Squadron Submarine COs entertained Ian Macintosh, the Captain SM, to dinner there when he was leaving. We had Lobster Thermidor, followed by the famous Duck, drinking Moet and Chandon champagne throughout our time at the Exeter Inn. Fortunately we had a minibus to transport us all. It was a very happy occasion.

We had a very happy period in our Married Quarter at Plymstock but now we had to go to pastures new as I was appointed to HMS *Osiris* then building at Barrow.

CHAPTER 12

HMS *Osiris* and Faslane

1963 to 1964

OSIRIS WAS A NEW 'O' CLASS SUBMARINE building at Barrow. It is wonderful to be going to a brand new submarine. Vickers at Barrow had a good reputation for submarine building and deservedly so. We rented a converted 'pigsty' and stable at Lakebank near the shore of Coniston Water in the Lake District. It was quite a distance from Barrow but amidst wonderful scenery in the country.

The conventional submarine building crew was using *Rifleman*, an old minesweeper, as their accommodation ship for offices, stores etc. I particularly remember *Valiant*'s launch when we were there and Mike LeFanu, then the Controller of the Navy, saying 'We can walk tall' at the lunch afterwards, as this was the first all British nuclear submarine.

Osiris was commissioned on 11 January 1964. Her number was 13 and she had S13 painted on the fin. She was the first submarine to be given this number since the sinking of K13 in the Gareloch in 1917. I was very determined that 13 should be our lucky number and at the commissioning I said 'I suppose our motto should be 'Unlucky for some, but not for us'. This did set the tone and she proved to be a very lucky and happy submarine. Our first Sea Inspection was on Friday 13th and we introduced the Friday Club Tie. You had to have dived in S13 on a Friday 13th to qualify. The tie was designed by my RP2 rating. Brian Baynham, Captain SM of the 3rd Squadron who did our inspection, was the first recipient. This tradition continued throughout the life of *Osiris*.

I had a great band of Officers, Tod Slaughter as First Lieutenant, Graham Baynes as the Marine Engineer, Hugh Michell as Navigator, Charlie Nixon-Eckersall as Torpedo Officer, Jeremy Dawson Hall as the Electrical Officer and Mike White of the Australian Navy as the 5th hand.

Author's wife cutting cake at commissioning of HMS Osiris, *1964*

The Commissioning and workup of a new submarine poses quite a few challenges even for experienced submariners. *Osiris* started off with a large number of her crew who were absolute newcomers. They all had to be trained in all the many aspects of their specific responsibilities and their duty to the safety of the submarine and their fellow crew members. The relatively short time between the start of sea trials and achieving operational capability meant a lot of work from my Officers and Senior Rates. It is a tribute to their expertise that we achieved the high standards required rapidly and cheerfully.

My former Radio Electrician has reminded me that I called for him to fix the radar. I was subsequently told that the 'tube' was defective and the submarine was not yet stored with a replacement. I sent him away smartly with instructions to 'make one'. He soon learnt that improvisation was a submariner's requirement! He eventually turned up with an impromptu 'A' display using the maintenance oscilloscope. He remembers this vividly some forty years later!

When the submarine was very new I managed to arrange a visit to the Holy Loch. This was the American base for their Polaris submarines with the depot ship, the USS *Hunley*. I said I was coming by boat and so *Osiris* arrived and berthed alongside the *Thomas Edison*. As far as I know this was the first occasion of a British submarine doing this. It was a great success and the American Chief Petty Officers had a great time drinking in the Senior Rates' Mess. There was an American Party for Officers and their wives in the big hall in Dunoon used by the US Navy. I was in conversation with one particularly pushy wife and travelled backwards the entire length of the hall during the evening!

During the visit there was a mutual admiration for items of the other's naval uniform so some serious swapping occurred. When the submarine sailed from Holy Loch it was nearly a question of asking the First Lieutenant to check the Ship's Company to ensure that the swaps had not included people as well as submarine sweaters, caps etc!

We fixed up an exercise with the *Edison* and got her to circle *Osiris* to see if we could detect her on our Type 186 sonar array. We did not. At the end of this jaunt with a Polaris submarine target, from their underwater telephone came the question 'What are your desires?' I sent back '36-23-36'. The next message from them said 'Do not understand 36-23-36'. We sent back 'You must have been away from port for a long time!'

We worked with the RAF flying Shackleton patrols from Bodo in Norway looking for Soviet submarines. We could call up an aircraft and direct it to investigate our contacts using a SubAir codebook. We did successfully vector an aircraft on to a snorting Russian Whisky class submarine. At the end of our time on patrol I sent a message, which read 'IHATESEX', this was the way the code was sent in two letter groups. I am afraid the RAF read more into this light-hearted message than intended as it partially indicated a percentage engine failure when decoded rather than the plain language intended!

I flew on one of these missions past North Cape and beyond on a ' Prudent Limit of Endurance Mission'. This meant many hours incarcerated in several thousand rivets flying in close formation. It was odd to take off in daylight and land back in daylight some 15

HMS Osiris, *Ship's Company*

hours or so later. Also the RAF did themselves proud so we consumed five meals during the mission.

By now we had developed the arts of going backwards and propelling with an evacuated control room as two minor enjoyments but possibly of little practical value, but you never know. We could now surface with an evacuated control room by another method of blowing air into the main ballast tanks as in the past this was only possible from the main blowing panel situated in the Control Room.

I spent a lot of time trying to develop a Type 197 plot to plot the active sonar transmissions detected by this intercept sonar. The object was to try and get some idea of their movement and to determine whether they were in contact. I regret to announce that with the best of intentions, and at one stage with two officers on this circular plot, we made no progress whatsoever!

In *Osiris* we developed the use of the Type 186 sonar plot, now called the Contact Evaluation Plot (CEP), almost as far as one could go within the limitations of the sonar and the plotting equipment. By now the CEP had been going a long time and the computer had to be harnessed to solve the equation later.

We took Captain (later Admiral) Tony Morton to sea with us for a Londonderry Exercise. He was about to become Captain (F) of a frigate squadron and to command HMS *Yarmouth*. It was good news that people now wanted to find out how submarines operated so that their ships would be better anti-submarine vessels. He is a most charming man and it was a pleasure to have him aboard. My path was to cross with his several times in the future. When he was driving *Yarmouth* HMS *Tiptoe* tried hard, and nearly succeeded, in sinking him by causing a lot of damage to the ship's hull by coming up underneath his ship in the Portland areas. Consequently when I was running the CO's Qualifying Course I found that *Yarmouth* was not at all keen to drive straight at the periscope to send my candidates deep. Therefore I cheekily sent him a signal saying 'One *Tiptoe* does not make an autumn'! It was Tony Morton who said to me that promotion came to those with a modicum of intelligence and who gave no trouble!

Tricia and I started off in a Married Quarter in Paisley and eventually moved into a new one in Bannachra Drive in Helensburgh. This was a very happy Married Patch and our children could play together happily and safely. The rating's Married Quarters were situated up a hill on the outskirts of Helensburgh. They were very isolated for the young wives especially if they had young children. The problem was that the Submarine Base at Faslane was expanding and no one knew quite what would happen in the future. I am not sure that the Planners at Helensburgh had much idea of what was about to happen up the road at Faslane!

Osiris, as a member of the 3rd Squadron, did not go south of Ailsa Craig in her first year, surely an indication of where operational interest was to be focused. However, you can have your cake and eat it! *Osiris* did a Home Port visit to Dundee. I found it to be a rather dull and uninteresting place but my sailors thought otherwise. The Dundee girls welcomed them with open arms, possibly because my chaps were much more attractive than the males in Dundee! Some of the crew would travel to Dundee from Faslane for a weekend after our visit. It does not take much imagination to figure out why.

So I handed over my Command to David Lund in Norway at Haakonsvern. He lived at No. 13 Bannachra Drive. I made my way home via a trip, at 20 knots, in HMS *Tiger* across the North Sea in some rough weather and ended up on the jetty at Rosyth absolutely frozen stiff whilst waiting for some transport to take me home after a very successful time in *Osiris*. She had an excellent Ship's Company who became very experienced and always trustworthy.

CHAPTER 13

Teacher COCOQC

March 1965 to April 1967

M Y NEXT JOB AFTER LEAVING *Osiris* was one of the most important in the Submarine Service: 'Teacher' to the Submarine Commanding Officers' Qualifying Course (the COCOQC). It is a challenging task but I always enjoyed it tremendously. I had immense faith in my appreciation of timing and range so it never worried me at all but I have to admit that nightly intakes of brandy provided much of the stamina required! Being 'Teacher' is really splendid for your eye and basically I do like to pass on my experience to others whether late at night over a glass or at the blackboard or even in the control room. That is why I enjoyed being at the Petty Officer's School at *Royal Arthur*.

There has been a tendency to glamorize the COs' course on TV and in books written by non-submariners. It is really just another course, admittedly a demanding one. The course is designed to teach the students how to be a Commanding Officer with the necessary emphasis on how to attack an enemy.

I can never forget and must record the very important part played by my Petty Officer Steward, PO Warden, who looked after my every need as well as ministering to the requirements of the 'Perishers', as the students were known. This was derived from the original Periscope Course and School. Petty Officer Warden was a doyen.

Although theoretically based at Faslane this job took me all over the place. The Course started with a four-week period at Fort Blockhouse at Gosport, using the Attack Teacher there. The appearance of a target in an Attack Teacher was not particularly realistic. However, it did allow people to get the feel and learn to appreciate range, course and speed of a target and then to manoeuvre into an attacking position. The students then switched to the Attack Teacher at Rothesay for Blind attack training e.g.

submarine v submarine. The Course also went to Londonderry where they visited the Joint Anti-Submarine School. They also visited various Naval Establishments and had many lectures by experts from various fields as well as me. There was also a period spent at sea off Londonderry attacking a submarine target.

One of the periods when exercising the submarine v submarine attack, a Soviet 'Whisky' class submarine was spotted by the Officer of the Watch in HMS *Finwhale*, then the submarine allocated to the COs' course. As the Russian interloper snorted by we formed up with *Finwhale* close astern and our proper target, an A class submarine on the Russian's quarter. Safety was not a problem as we could see the wake of our fellow trailer quite clearly. We kept this up for a few hours until we ran out of our allocated area and let the Russian blithely carry on!

After all this came the really serious bit of the course, the seagoing weeks in the Clyde, when after sailing from Faslane on Monday morning in the submarine allocated to the Perisher we spent the daylight hours attacking surface ships, returning onshore at night to a hotel in Rothesay. The submarine either anchored or secured to a buoy. The number of ships gradually increased from one in the first week, to two in the second week and thence up to five in the final week. The speed of ships gradually increased during the week until reaching maximum on the Friday. It was possible to get over 20 runs in on a fast day, exhausting but great fun. The students had to learn to develop what is called a 'periscope eye' and awareness of the proximity and movement of ships around them, going deep for safety reasons when in close proximity, and then returning to periscope depth, when safe to do so, and carrying on the attack if possible.

It was usual to have a party on the Thursday evening to allow the students to let their hair down and meet the Officers from the target ships. There was an ulterior motive! A suitably tired chap on the Friday morning was a very good example of how someone exhausted would react to the pressure of a fast moving situation.

All this had to be carried out in a professional manner exercising full control of the submarine. I spent a lot of time getting people to develop an automatic reaction to the importance of checking the trim depth speed and sonar picture etc before putting up the

Commanding Officer CO's Qualifying Course, Frigate at 850 yards 1965

periscope to take a target observation. Eventually this all becomes second nature to the Captain of a submarine. A ship cannot fly and travels only 900 yards at 30 knots in a minute yet there was always a tendency to want to have a quick look for reassurance by the students and they had to be taught to resist the temptation to have a quick look solely to reassure themselves that the target was still there!

The stopwatch became an essential factor in safety and the students learnt to love their stopwatch. Time is exact and if their range estimate was also exact they could easily determine when it was safe to come to periscope depth, after a run towards the target, or when to take the next look, or even when they might have to go deep to duck under an escort. We should all learn from our mistakes and when possible I let them make the error! One example was when I let a chap return to periscope depth inside the turning circle of a Dutch destroyer. He got the shock of his life when he put the periscope up and saw the destroyer at 450 yards! Another took a bad range and hared towards a frigate that turned towards. We had a closing speed of 38 knots; he too got a shock when he put the periscope up. My treasured stopwatch is now an exhibit in the Submarine Museum at Gosport.

During the sea weeks in the Clyde I awaited the horoscope for the day from the *Scottish Daily Express*, looking for the day's horoscope for Aries as it decided how the day would proceed. Some thought this a joke! It may have started that way but they will never know!

Although much emphasis was rightly placed on 'attacking' a target safely much else had to be taught and exercised. I was constantly concerned at the lack of submarine operating knowledge exhibited by my students. Many of them did not appear to have picked up this vital know-how en route to the course. The need for precision navigation when inshore and in shallow water was ever present in my mind. Ship recognition was also important, as is the ability to make reasonable estimates of its range on first sighting. I started to get students interested in Merchant Ship recognition with the numbers then around in the Clyde. The estimates of tonnage of some of these monsters were widely out.

I introduced a little exercise called 'Roundabout' to teach people inshore work, periscope reconnaissance, intelligence gathering and minelaying during the summer months when there was the second NATO course running concurrently. The second course reduced the number of target runs available, as the target ships had to run past two submarines a few miles apart before repeating the next run. As an example a summer Perisher might produce a low of 280 sea attacks as opposed to a high rate of some 330 in a good spring. Much depended on the type of targets allocated as fast ships were often in short supply!

The course always ended with a 48-hour exercise called 'Cockfight'. At the end of the last week the course could be attacking the Depot Ship escorted by three or four frigates. Practice torpedoes might be fired if there was time, but usually one day a week was allowed for that in the preceding weeks. The exercise consisted of simulated minelays, special operations such as intelligence gathering, evasion of a patrolling frigate, or perhaps a periscope recce of the shore night and day. By this time it was decided who had passed.

One of my unenviable tasks was to pass or fail students; always difficult when you are aware that it would have a serious effect on an Officer's future career since he would have to leave submarines. I really had a very simple yardstick. Was he safe or could he leave 69 widows and lots of orphans on the jetty (69 being the complement of an O class submarine then)? I only had one student who genuinely lacked a periscope eye; he could look through the periscope and just not see a ship as he swung round. Fortunately he recognized this. Others had to be failed because they just did not make the grade when it came to getting and retaining the picture. I always explained my reasons for failures to Captain SM and he always supported my view. Captain SM came out with the submarine to observe the students in action during the straight forward attacking part of the proceedings in the final exercise. I usually managed to explain the reasons to those who failed, some accepted, some did not but that was to be expected. All I can say is that those who I had passed never let me down and many went on to higher things. I had 27 successful candidates and eight failures. This ratio was about right although my failure rate was a little unbalanced by having to fail two Canadian Officers, largely because their appointing had not prepared them for either Command or this demanding course.

The sea weeks could be tiring, as I had to be in the Control Room for many hours. I can therefore give a big vote of thanks to brandy and cigars! I suppose there is nothing more annoying than being buttonholed by COs asking after their ex First Lieutenants and when told they were not up to it and not doing at all well, said that they had had their reservations. It was a pity that they recommended the poor chap in the first place and let him expect something really beyond his reach as well as inflicting the strains of the course on him. Certainly it was a waste of my time!

Once upon a time I could tell you a minute's passage of time to a second's accuracy without a stopwatch as I had lived by the minute's run (the obligatory go deep criteria for safety versus a surface ship). Those days are long past even though the memories of this very exacting but enjoyable appointment are still fresh in my memory after all these years. One saying that reflected some of my teaching stems from the card game of bridge 'one peep's worth two finesses'. This message is engraved on a silver ashtray given to me by one of my courses with the word 'Gotcher' in the centre!

I was amused to read that Terry Woods, one of my ex students, when he was 'Teacher' was using the submarine's bell to announce errors to his students and to send them a bit demented. Actually I think he was doing it incorrectly! I used the bell as an 'aggression bell' and rang it when they were just sitting there and not closing the target's track. If they continually wanted to look through the periscope I sent them off on errands like asking the chap on watch in the torpedo compartment what his name was. If they came back panting and still determined to have a peep, I sent them back to find out whether he was married. The mad chef with a meat cleaver running amok through the control room was a somewhat misplaced diversion as this played no part in teaching people how to attack. It had its origins in Sea Inspection ploys as it was something different and added a bit of humour when things were getting a bit too serious.

Now that the diesel submarine has disappeared from the RN's order of battle and the course is now concerned with nuclear submarine command the emphasis had to change. The quick close range visual attack was no longer relevant. However, the ability to operate at periscope depth with many ships around still requires the ability to develop a sound periscope eye. The emphasis on navigation, the safe conduct of the submarine, the ability to plan for operations and the many other facets of submarine operations that face the Captain of a nuclear submarine have to be taught and exercised.

Our youngest son, Peter, was born in January 1967, so I was once again a father after a longish gap! His Christening on board HMS *Maidstone* in the Captain's cabin was a little embarrassing. He yelled throughout whilst baby Wadman, the Commander SM's new arrival, was as good as gold! It was fun to have a dual Christening for the offspring of these two ageing fathers.

So I turned over to Sandy Woodward after my two-year stint. I gather that he found his first courses demanding.

CHAPTER 14

Commander SM Seventh Squadron Singapore

September 1967 to April 1969

A VERY HAPPY TIME WAS TO BE experienced in Singapore. Since I had been in the Far East as a midshipman I knew what to expect. There was HMS *Forth* as the depot ship and she had of course been the depot ship in the Med during my service in *Sturdy* and *Trump*.

We lived very comfortably at Number 1 Hawkins Road, Rimau, within the Naval Base. The house, which had been used as a brothel by the Japanese, had verandahs, shutters and fans but no air-conditioning. The Base was kept immaculately, with the grass continually mowed by teams of men with large lethal-looking petrol driven strimmers. The Monsoon drains were sprayed with oil to prevent mosquito larvae hatching. Our gardens grew orchids and camellias. There was a moonflower in a pot by the front door, which opened for just one night giving off a glorious perfume. In contrast our 'paper bag' tree grew durian fruit which have a disgusting smell. In the small valley below the house tall trees provided nesting sites for sea eagles (these birds were featured on the $5 Singapore stamps).

The squadron consisted of A class streamline submarines, *Rorqual*, a Porpoise class, and *Onslaught* from the O class. The A boats had little air conditioning and were very hot inside once dived.

I had sufficient experience of submarine squadrons now to know exactly how I saw my job as Commander SM. It is a strange position as technically one is Second in Command of the squadron but the Commander of the Depot Ship is 2 i/c of her and he would not be a submarine specialist. Basically Commander SM is responsible for everything to do with the submarines, training, operational state, morale and so on. I considered that I should spend as much time at sea in the submarines as possible. Fortunately four of the boats were

103

commanded by ex students from my 'Teacher' days. The Staff Officer Operations (SOO) was also an old student so we knew each other well.

Ken Martin left as Captain SM soon after my arrival and he was relieved by Lance Bell Davies, whom I knew well. Indeed he had been the Officers' Training Officer during my submarine training. He was also an ex 'Teacher' and had been the Captain of HMS *Leander* when I was CO of *Artful* and we had exercised with his ship in Derry waters.

I travelled around, with visits to Australia, where there was still a British Submarine presence although the Australians were now acquiring their own 'O' boats. Their COs and submarine staff were all ex British who had now emigrated to Australia, and I knew them all very well. I also went to Bangkok, Hong Kong and Yokosuka, where the Americans had a submarine base.

Forth left Singapore for a longish period when she became the Fleet's Maintenance ship at Mombasa when the British were giving up Aden. The small submarine staff left in Singapore was the rear link and had the additional task of fielding any wives' problems. My SOO used to say I was the Chief Wren Welfare. There were no great problems and I enjoyed the challenge. I used to visit the hospital once a week to see any submariners who had been hospitalized.

Life in the Naval Base centred on the Officers' Club where there was a good swimming pool, plenty of Tiger Beer and delicious chips; just the place to take a young family.

The only trouble with Singapore is that there is no sense of changing seasons. It is so near the Equator that the days are of the same length, and it gets dark at the same time every day of the year. There is very little twilight. In the monsoon season torrential rain used to fall at 4 o'clock every afternoon. This did help to cool the rather sweaty and oppressive atmosphere.

I spent a lot of my time trying to make the wire-guided electrically propelled Mk 23 torpedo work! In spite of the most intensive work by all concerned, including the double preparation of the torpedo by the Depot Ship staff, and the double jointing of the watertight joint of the guidance wire, there was total failure. It was a rotten torpedo, being just a Mk20 with a guidance wire dispenser attached. Quite how it was ever accepted into service is beyond me. At this stage little interest was shown by Head Office as the Mk24 was coming along, it was to prove another nightmare weapon! We had an excellent Squadron sports period with various trophies for a variety of 'games'.

I cannot remember exactly when HMS *Cachalot* joined the Squadron, which had been much depleted when *Auriga* and *Anchorite* sailed for home going opposite ways round the world to the UK.

Rorqual was one of those submarines bedevilled by bad luck. During her life she had all sorts of problems, and here in Singapore, she had major engine defects to rectify. I spent a lot of time being a shoulder to cry on, particularly by the Engineers. After many weeks in harbour she eventually got to sea, although she managed to run aground during a simulated minelay during my sea inspection, which I conducted after her workup after such a long period in harbour. The Staff ashore wanted to know why I did not have a Board of Inquiry! I laughed it off as one of those things as *Rorqual* had had enough on her plate. I wonder why Naval Shore Staffs want to do everything by the book, when they should be well aware that the sea is quite a different element!

One of the Squadron's legacies was a hangover from the Confrontation with Indonesia. Bigger and better methods of landing SBS Royal Marines were experimented with, including modified torpedoes and breathing from air supplies rigged in pipes around the fin. Quite frankly I found these gadgets very dangerous, and when we endeavoured to show them to the Commander in Chief, they failed miserably. So much so that I was able to discontinue this dangerous waste of submarine time.

When Admiral McGeoch, as Flag Officer Submarines, visited Singapore, we gave him a Chinese meal. In order that he would meet as many people as possible in this large Chinese restaurant, I thought it would be a good idea to change places between courses so that he would have different people to talk to for each course. This was not a good idea, as the table became chaotic with piles of food everywhere!

I have particularly happy memories of my trip to Sydney by submarine! I started off in *Onslaught* and then switched to *Cachalot*

Commander SM, Exercise Coral Sands 1968

by transferring in a rubber dinghy in the Java Sea. I was to ride *Cachalot* for Exercise 'Coral Sands', a rather grand SEATO Exercise.

Andy Buchanan, one of my ex students, commanded *Cachalot*. I kept watch, one in three, throughout the exercise as a watchkeeping officer with Tony Steiner, a great cartoonist. Our Contact Evaluation Plot was a work of art with oranges walking all over it as we were on the orange side. I prided myself that I had not forgotten how to start and stop snorting as OOW.

On our arrival in Sydney I could not be bothered to wait for some Australian immigration official to give the all clear. The Aussies are awfully fussy about people arriving from other countries! He was not amused to see me making off. It was the first country that I have visited in a submarine and had to face an Immigration chap. Surely this was a load of nonsense!

The Staff Officers and Submarine COs took Flag Officer Submarines, Admiral Mike Pollock, on a run ashore in Sydney. We kicked off with drinks at the Royal Sydney Yacht Club, from there to supper at an 'old time music hall' where, whilst eating, it was the done thing to chiack the actors in a play called 'Her Only Mistake'.

Men diners had to wear black cardboard moustaches. It was hilarious, as was the repartee. From the Music Hall we moved on to the 'Whisky a GoGo', this was a strip joint with go-go dancers. It was difficult to get the Admiral to leave. Thence back to the HMS *Forth* for drinks in the cuddy (the Captain's cabin). What a night!

I remember ending up the next day in the American submarine *Jallao* rather late at night. She was last of the US diesel boats and I think that she was an unmodified Fleet submarine. We drank all the 'medicinal' brandy, as all the US ships are 'dry'. The CO was quite a character and obviously not of the Rickover Breed. He gave me a 'Diesel Boats Forever Badge' that allowed you to display your previous service in the diesel submarines by means of stars. There were not enough spaces for me!

On the way back to Singapore I decided to forsake alcohol for a couple of weeks just to prove I could. This was much to Lance Bell Davies' distaste and he kept on trying to get me to have the odd gin and tonic. On arrival at Singapore we stayed at sea for the Sea Inspection by the Chief of Staff to the Commander Far East Fleet. Lance had a big giggle by producing a Chinese guard from all the Chinese ratings onboard, mainly cooks and stewards! They received the Admiral complete with a three-piece Chinese band. Actually they were very well trained and smart and much enjoyed the whole

HMS Forth, *Chinese Guard 1968*

charade! After the inspection I came off the wagon. First there were lots of drinks with Lance, then to the Chief Petty Officers' mess where I consumed quite a lot, as they were very hospitable. So I arrived home next day with an almighty hangover, so much for my TT period! Lance left shortly afterwards and was relieved by Jimmy Launders, a distinguished CO from World War II and therefore much older than us lot. He had sunk two U–Boats, one of them submerged.

I still treasure the cartoon drawing of me produced by *Cachalot* entitled 'Our Beloved Leader', on the lines of Big Brother (from the book *1984* I suspect), with my 'Thoughts' underneath. They were: 'The Best is the Enemy of the Good', 'Time is Exact', 'Discard the Nugatory', and 'Polish'. I think the sentiments are still applicable today and perhaps one or two of our Politicians could adopt these watchwords! I still have the 'Coral Sands Medal' that they presented to me.

I was rather sad to leave this happy appointment but the Squadron was running down and was soon to leave Singapore completely. I was bound for a new appointment in command of a Nuclear Submarine.

We had a nightmare flight home with RAF planes breaking down all over place. We even had to land back in Singapore after take-off for some reason, jettisoning a full load of fuel before returning. After take-off the next day there lay more troubles ahead. Nevertheless, in spite of everything we got back to England on the Thursday night having 'left' Singapore theoretically on the Monday evening. There was even a mix up with my car, which was not awaiting me as the RAF at Brize Norton had not told the driver when the aircraft was expected, so he had driven all the way back to Portsmouth! It was some hours before we arrived at Tricia's parents' home in Charmouth!

CHAPTER 15

Nuclear Course, Staff Course, HMS *Courageous* at Barrow and PISCES

Nuclear Course at Royal Naval College Greenwich

I HAD TO ATTEND TWO COURSES before taking up my appointment to *Courageous*, then being built at Barrow. I am not wild about courses! However, the most important task was to find somewhere to live. Thanks to a very understanding Married Quarters Officer at HMS *Warrior*, the Naval Command Headquarters, at Northwood, I was allocated a new quarter at Hillingdon on the outskirts of Uxbridge. This meant that I would have to set off early to drive to Greenwich and drive back late. I had to try hard to cope with the mathematics used in Nuclear Physics. Quite why a non Engineer had to cope with the vagaries of complicated nuclear physics was rather beyond me. The teaching at Greenwich was rather in a groove and did not take kindly to any suggestion about their course, taking it as a personal criticism. They did not like me starting my own notebook rather than keeping to the handout for one section, even though I had carefully glued the various bits and pieces into my own personal and fully detailed notebook. Such is life in the academic world, rather divorced from the world we live in. Later on my friend at the Ministry of Defence told me that I had received a 'bad report' from Greenwich even though I did pass out 'Top' of my Nuclear Course. My wristwatch had a radioactive luminous dial and hands, and sent the Geiger counter wild when we conducted an experiment.

Joint Services Staff Course

It was appropriate that leave between appointments was known as gardening leave. We bought our first house in Chesham Bois, in Buckinghamshire, so that it would be handy for a base and close to the Joint Services Staff Course at Latimer. It was a new house and we had to develop a garden from a building site. Also we had none of the furniture required so thanks to the Harrods sale and sundry other places we managed to equip our house very comfortably before starting the course at Latimer.

The Joint Services Staff Course was an experience. The course was designed to broaden the outlook of officers, not only in the military field, but also their understanding of those factors that determine and subsequently affect military thought. Officers of many nations and services assembled together for six months in this 'hothouse'. We were taught the ins and outs of Staff Work. I regret that I did not take it at all seriously! There were four distinct periods during the Course. Think pink was the watchword as pink paper was used for the staff answer to the various problems we were set. I deliberately 'thought pink' in periods one and three and pleased myself in periods two and four. I am glad to say that this rather flummoxed the Staff, much to my amusement. There was such a lack of adventurous thinking available. After my allotted study of Communist dominance in South East Asia I wrote off Cambodia and Laos. My extensive research proved to be completely wrong, having been gleaned from all the books in the library.

The one project I really enjoyed was early on, called Exercise Zhivago. The task was to determine the most effective foreign and defence policies for the USSR to pursue in the years 1970 to 1980. I made much of the opportunity to write as a Russian and used my language knowledge to dress up the final discourse. The staff awarded me an Order of Lenin for this task.

It was very interesting to mix with so many different people. At one Mess Dinner a Pakistani team: a wing commander, a naval commander and a major, surrounded me. They gave me instruction about Kashmir throughout the meal!

There was an American Artilleryman in our group, very experienced with two periods in Vietnam. He was great fun. His dress uniform was hilarious as it did credit to the Doorman at a great London Hotel.

A trip to the RAF V Bomber base gave me the chance to talk down a V bomber as the Air Traffic Controller. It was fun to have the illusion of taking charge of landing this large aircraft with the rest of my syndicate aboard.

There were a number of external visits, which helped to break up the grind of the paper warfare of the course, and a seemingly endless supply of lectures. I am sure that the time at Latimer made me more knowledgeable, but I must confess that I cannot recollect using any of the knowledge gained.

We had one external trip abroad during the Course and I chose Berlin. It was absolutely fascinating to see the 'Wall', pass through 'Check Point Charlie' (in uniform, as servicemen of the occupying powers had free access to the various sectors), and see the Soviet war memorial in East Berlin. This was a very sombre and forbidding place as the Russians lost so many soldiers in the assault on Berlin at the war's end. There was also the opportunity to see the Brandenburg Gate and the Unter den Linden. The shops and nightlife in West Berlin were a marked contrast to the East. The East German border guards abounded, and were as curious about us as we were about them. I was thankful that the Staff Course let me home every night but glad when it came to an end.

One major lesson from this course was learnt from the very impressive American General who was Supreme Allied Commander Europe (SACEUR). He said during his lecture 'You are either on the Upgrade or the Downgrade'. This is a very useful signpost to how life should be lived, as it implies that there is no state of equilibrium!

Sir John Wolfenden gave a very interesting lecture. At question time after the lecture an RAF Officer asked Sir John 'What are the most difficult ages for women?' Sir John, who had many daughters, quickly replied 'Between 14 and 40!' There was much laughter!

HMS *Courageous* at Barrow

To someone who had worked his way up in Diesel Boats, the Command of a Nuclear Submarine was pure gold, and so it proved. For one thing it was back to Vickers at Barrow and also another brand new submarine with all the challenges that entails. I had gone up to Barrow to see *Courageous* launched whilst doing the Joint Staff Course and met most of my future Officers. I had an excellent bunch. It was said at one time that I had fixed my team. Nothing could be further from the truth! It was not common knowledge that

HMS Courageous, *Launch 1970*

I had been offered *Conqueror* originally. She was actually scheduled to complete building some six months before *Courageous*. However, as far as I was concerned *Conqueror* was a Cammel Lairds boat, and I wanted a Vickers built one! Luck was again on my side, as in the end *Courageous* completed before *Conqueror*, because some idiot had sabotaged her gearbox towards the end of her construction. We always had a friendly rivalry with 'Conks' and they came to Barrow for a Sports Day, which was great fun. *Conqueror* also had a fine team of officers. Richard Sharpe was the Executive Officer (the second in Command) and Mike Boyce was their Sonar Officer (a future Chief of the Defence Staff). It was to be poetic justice that Richard Sharpe commanded *Courageous* towards the end of her First Commission!

Once again I stress the importance of melding a Ship's Company together whilst building or indeed refitting. Much thought has to be given to this and I was fortunate to have David Wixon (the Marine Engineering Officer and Senior Technical Officer) and Paddy O'Riordan as the Executive Officer (also a future Admiral). They organized that *Courageous* had a Home Port visit to Newcastle by coach (an unheard of venture as homeport visits were rewards for seagoing vessels!). We had a memorable visit although I made one big gaff. I presented a crest to the Sunderland RNA but I referred to them as the Newcastle RNA. I was not familiar with the local geography, and certainly unaware of the intense rivalry between Newcastle and Sunderland!

The Barrow to Keswick walk resulted in a cup for *Courageous* with the winning team. A West Country tour of naval establishments with a musical show about nuclear submarines written and composed by David Wixon among others was organized. It was called 'What's in a Name' and we visited HMS *Royal Arthur*, Manadon (the Engineer's Academy) and HMS *Raleigh* (the new entry training establishment) and HMS *Drake*. The Manadon show was a bit of a disaster as half our cast failed to turn up on time. The Coxswain got lost (so he said!) and I was not amused! Nevertheless it was a successful tour and in March 1972 we did another tour, then to HMS *Mercury* (the Communications School) and HMS *Collingwood* (the Electrical School). These trips did much to make us all of one company.

Apart from finding out about *Courageous* I kept myself busy.

October 1970: Wilton Park

In October 1970 I was fortunate to attend a Wilton Park 'Conference', having applied for a place following an Admiralty Fleet Order (AFO) which invited applications. Wilton Park is a grand country house near Steyning in Sussex. The theme of their 125th Conference was 'The United States and Europe'. A conference there is international, and was attended by a multi-national group of people, with a diversity of interests and experience, roughly in the 30–40 age group but some being much older

Fifteen nations can partake in these conferences and all are members of the OECD. At this conference twelve nations were represented. The Foreign and Commonwealth Office footed 85% of the costs.

There were a number of lectures and discussion groups with outside visits, which included the House of Commons, Windsor, Hampton Court and Imperial College as well as some London theatre productions. It was a welcome change to be away from the naval environment, and have the opportunity to meet some delightful people. The country house atmosphere with no exams, good food, afternoons 'off' to visit locally, and evening lectures from various experts, provided me with a most enjoyable holiday. Lectures, talks and discussions were held in three languages. English, French and German simultaneous translation was provided through headphones for lectures and talks. I well remember Enoch Powell visiting for an evening talk and his unique language ability as he took questions in French and German and answered them in the appropriate language. We were encouraged to attend various discussion groups and in order to show willing (and with some considerable assistance) I addressed the French group to lead a discussion on 'Youth Today'. My French tuition had been abandoned at the age of 15 when I took up Russian in preference to French at Dartmouth and my pronunciation was, and still is, terrible, but I did get some encouraging applause.

The lecturers were very experienced and senior people and ranged from ex-ministers to important civil servants. Various political flavours were represented, especially the British, French and American. The Confederation of British Industry's Director General gave a good talk, and covered political as well as economic considerations. Speakers were generally limited to 30 minutes, and thereafter the questions and discussion had a time limit of one and a half hours. Then there was a 'therapeutic' break in the proceedings. It was a great privilege to hear such a varied collection of lectures and I still have the notes that I took.

I made friends with two Americans, Virginia Page from California and Bob Teitelman, an attorney from Boston, and corresponded with them for some time afterwards. I have an abiding memory of our final dinner where I had been 'elected' to make the farewell speech on behalf of the 'students'. Fortunately the staff had sufficient foibles to be 'taken off' and I had the right props to carry it through successfully.

PISCES

Whilst standing by my submarine I carried out an appraisal, on behalf of Flag Officer Submarines, of the submersible PISCES, which had been developed by Vickers at Barrow. A separate Company called Vickers Oceanics operated it. The support ship was called Vickers *Venturer* and had a massive A frame to launch the submersibles. Pisces was supposed to be designed for a variety of tasks. These were cable fixing and maintenance, pipeline surveys, torpedo recovery and underwater searches. One of the enthusiastic team was Bob Easthaugh, who appeared to be a Jack of all Trades, assisting in everything from repairing the sonar to launching the Pisces vehicle. I accompanied Vickers *Venturer* up to the Clyde and did a dive in Pisces to the bottom of the Arran trench, a depth of over a 100 fathoms. I did not see much down there except one large fish. You had to wrap up with plenty of warm clothing as it was very cold inside Pisces when diving deep. The submersible worked but there were a number of problems as far as I could see. The after-sphere, which was an essential part of the design, could flood up unnoticed, as there was no sensor. If this happened there was no ability to get to the surface without assistance, as the machine would be negatively buoyant. I believe this did happen later and it was only the ability of another submersible close by to assist that enabled the stricken one to return to the surface. That incident was in very deep water off the Bahamas.

Pisces had no reliable or efficient sonar. The set that I saw was primitive and did not appear to produce any results of value as far as I could see. Whilst the vehicle was at the forefront of its design then, I thought it was completely underfunded and lacked essential safety features.

I believe it was later developed into a useful project, but I was never thanked for my report by the Director of the Oceanics Department! It is interesting to note that a Pisces III was later trapped on the seabed at 1575 feet after it had been damaged during a recovery operation following a normal dive. The crew of two were trapped on the seabed for 76 hours and rescued finally with very little air left to breathe. The full story of the rescue was told in a book by the senior 'pilot', who was an ex-submariner, Roger Chapman. The title of the book, appropriately, was *No Time on our Side*.

CHAPTER 16

HMS *Courageous* 1970 to 1973

Building the Submarine

IT IS A MISTAKE TO APPOINT the major part of a Ship's Company too early to a submarine being built. There is not sufficient work to keep them occupied and we all know what happens to idle hands. Unfortunately the build often takes longer than forecast. In the case of a nuclear submarine, whilst there is much for the crew to learn before first going to sea for Contractor's Sea Trials (CSTs), it is essential to keep them gainfully occupied.

Fortunately we did not have too much trouble with the junior ratings living the life of Riley ashore in digs (called Approved Lodgings). I often wonder why the ratings think that Officers are oblivious of what goes on. I did adopt a method of punishment which was more in keeping with modern times. Those misdemeanours which would have attracted stoppage of leave were awarded fairly hefty fines. Being hit in the pocket always hurt and taught a lesson to be remembered. I really had very few 'defaulters' during my time in *Courageous*.

There was a large wooden mock-up of a nuclear submarine at Barrow which could be used to acquaint people with the layout and placement of various engineering systems. It also aided the Vickers personnel to place items in the best way possible given the constraints of the space available as well as interference with other bits and pieces. From time to time the submarine's crew would suggest a better solution or request an additional item. It was then up to the resident Naval Overseer to see if it was feasible and not too expensive. It was always best to have a good working relationship with both the builder, Vickers, and the constructors who represented the Director General Submarines' department at Bath.

As the Captain, it was necessary to rely heavily on the Officers to ensure that things progress smoothly. I had such a good crowd of people in *Courageous* that I could sit back and let it all happen. The

Officers had a busy time organizing their men as well as arranging courses and instruction. In addition the junior Officers had to acquaint themselves fully with the submarine and were examined by the First Lieutenant and the Senior Technical Officers in order to ensure that they reached a high standard.

I had to make myself familiar with every nook and cranny. I particularly remember sitting on top of the nuclear reactor and looking up and around at the massive space that formed the Reactor Compartment. I can assure you that once the reactor is shut down it is quite safe to enter the compartment after a relatively short interval! One Sunday afternoon I was clambering around the submarine in my white overalls and went down into the small compartment which housed the electrolyser. This was the vital equipment for generating oxygen to replace that used by the crew. There were two Vickers engineers there so I asked them what they were doing. They said 'Did I want an honest reply?' Of course I said 'Yes'. 'Honestly', they said, 'as little as possible!' I was not too impressed, but it did reflect modern attitudes to work and rewards!

It was decided to have a garden party at David Wixon's house. An American Submarine, the USS *Sirago*, was in Barrow on the day so we invited them to join us. The Officers dressed up in the correct rig, wearing white trousers with their normal naval uniform. The wives and girl friends wore their summer dresses and colourful hats. The mayor of Barrow came and cut the cake. There was only one snag, a fairly major one, it poured with rain throughout! Our band was forced to take cover in the garage. I am not sure that our guests knew there was a band. The American Officers were slightly bemused by the whole affair. The lasses' dresses soaked up the rain. However, it remains a very happy memory.

Contractor's Sea Trials (CSTs)

The start and end of CSTs were very much determined by the depth of water both on sailing and return. The Navigating Officer, Nigel Goodwin, and I did a recce. We made a mistake by checking out the channel at low water. The tidal range is large at Barrow. It is as much as 32 feet and as the draught of *Courageous* was some 26 feet, our survey of the channel to the sea was hardly reassuring!

These trials lasted some 50 days. The submarine flies the red ensign and in effect I was the ship's Master being employed by Vickers. It was traditional for Vickers to 'pay' a shilling a day and I have a framed cheque for my time on CSTs. The trials were conducted with a mix of Vickers' engineers and workers and my Ship's Company.

The first part consisted of Beam Pattern Trials for the large bow mounted sonar, Type 2001, and were conducted in Loch Striven with the submarine moored between buoys. Then after a short self workup we did a deep dive. There followed extensive self noise trials moored between buoys at Inverary. A very boring but very necessary period.

The eggbeater (the slang name for the outboard motor contraption that could be used to drive the stern one way or the other when manoeuvring in harbour) did not work during CSTs, nor for many months after Commissioning. This was very irritating. However, when it did we could at last berth alongside without tugs.

It was a busy period with many transfers of Vickers and Ministry of Defence personnel. The food was always excellent as Vickers provided it and their standard was much higher than the normal naval scale. I had a particular problem as I developed clusters of blisters on the soles of my feet. They exuded an infectious liquid and had to be punctured and dressed by my very attentive doctor, as we had a Surgeon Lieutenant onboard by then. It was a useful period to get to grips with living and working onboard but had little to do with submarining.

Commissioning

Mike Gregory, my Communications Officer (a future Admiral and Flag Officer Scotland), organized the Commissioning. He compiled a brief history of ships that had borne the name. We toyed with the idea of inviting the German CO of the U-boat that sunk the Aircraft Carrier *Courageous* in 1940. However, Flag Officer Submarines warned us off this idea! We had a sprinkling of survivors of the old *Courageous* at the commissioning ceremony. Mrs Mckeig-Jones, the widow of the Captain, who went down with his ship, came. She was a really charming lady and extremely interested in the submarine that was now to bear the name.

Author's wife cutting cake at commissioning of HMS Courageous, *1971*

Mrs Morris, the wife of John Morris, a Labour Party Minister of Defence (Equipment), who had launched the submarine, attended with her family. She has kept in touch with the submarine throughout its life. John Morris is now Lord Morris of Aberavon.

The Commissioning day passed in a flash. It was a very successful day. Tricia came up to Barrow and assisted the youngest crew-member in the traditional cutting of the cake. She wore the same hat at the final 'paying off' ceremony 21 years later. It was noteworthy that the same chap assisted the last Captain's wife with cutting their cake, but he was now a seasoned Petty Officer Cook.

On leaving for Faslane to join our Squadron I thought that the pilot was doing his best to put us aground as he made insufficient allowance for the tidal stream. He took us well to starboard of the correct track but we ensured that we altered back to a safer place!

Workup

The workup of *Courageous* was not particularly memorable. The Squadron Staff did not have any real experience of the ways of a nuclear submarine apart from the nuclear engineering requirements. Consequently although we sampled quite a lot of the various requirements I could not wait for the operational practice that we required.

We were all very conscious of the dangers posed by flooding whilst deep and the remedial actions required in order to avoid a disaster like that of the US Navy's *Thresher*. This meant constant vigilance whilst deep and going fast as well as plenty of practice in emergency procedures. This practice involved remedial measures causing large bow down angles and then large bow up angles. During our workup the bow down angle achieved was sufficient to cause a torpedo to slip in its cradle! It was also necessary to get people used to the large angles of heel achieved when using a lot of helm to change course especially as this would occur if we had to evade torpedoes. The submarine would do a 'snap roll' and send everything flying. When using what was called 'angles and dangles' for practice we made sure that everything was battened down and everyone was made aware of what to expect.

During the workup when working with HMS *Hermione* we had to transfer a Petty Officer using her Wasp helicopter, as he required medical attention. The sea was quite rough and the spectacular photograph of the helicopter hovering just above the small amount of visible fin appeared in the National Press.

HMS Courageous, *1972, helicopter transfer of sick rating*

I am not sure that the 3rd Submarine Squadron staff appreciated our sense of humour. We were always somewhat scornful about the new oil employed in the hydraulic systems. It was called PR 1192 and had some special attribute of being able to absorb a lot of water yet still work as a hydraulic fluid. It leaked everywhere and white shirts took on a brownish hue. It was said to be a good handcream and hair tonic by those of us who spent time at the periscope.

The underway noise trials were conducted on the Rona range. This required us to proceed deep at high speed for a large number of runs without the benefit of accurate navigation. The submarine had to reverse course at the end of each run with a mere 5 degrees of wheel in order to avoid dropping speed as well as ensuring that we did not have an endless succession of snap rolls. There was a rather primitive method of keeping track of our position on shore. This was meant to help us navigate safely. I regarded the whole operation as fraught with danger and made my views known!

Operational Factors

I have called this section Operational Factors as they were very important and had to be understood and negotiated in order to achieve the standards required.

The Type 2001 sonar had a chequered history in our nuclear submarines. It had been designed as a powerful active sonar. It had been utilized to defend the fleet from submarine attack by using a link ship to relay submarine detections to the Force Commander. The drill was cumbersome and the underwater communications subject to problems. In many ways it was a very theoretical concept as any attacking submarine would be alerted early on to the Force's presence. The powerful sonar transmissions could be intercepted many miles away so they could act as a homing beacon! The concept was attractive to anyone who needed to persuade someone to spend money on expensive nuclear submarines.

Fortunately, there was a fairly good passive capability and the active detection took a back seat as the Royal Navy was much more interested in establishing the ability to detect other nuclear submarines at a respectable range whilst utilizing our nuclear submarines in the anti-submarine role.

The performance of the sonar in the passive role was downgraded by flow noise caused by water flowing over the dome that housed the sonar array. This meant that the submarine's speed was limited to quite a low speed if required to detect or hold quiet targets. Until the so called 'chin strap' placement of the dome in the *Swiftsure* Class we had to do the best we could. A fibreglass dome was fitted over the array eventually and this markedly increased the ability to hold contacts at a higher speed than hitherto. Personally, I think that far too much was expected from the 2001's passive capability. The towed array, that was introduced much later, produced a huge gain in initial detection range as well as the ability to classify a detection.

Another limitation was reception of the submarine broadcast. Use of the fin-mounted aerials limited the submarine to periscope depth in order to read the broadcast. The only other method was to use the ALK buoy. This was called the Borstal Boy by us, as it was prone to go AWOL! It had to be reeled in and out from its stowage in the casing. Once it was streamed the submarine was speed limited as otherwise the cable would break. We always used to say that the Soviets must have collected lots of these buoys! It was not until the 'Floating Wire Aerial' was introduced that a satisfactory solution was achieved. Even then, until a reelable aerial was fitted, it was quite a task to stream the aerial from the back of the fin. A slow turn was required to ensure that the aerial did not get chopped. Once dived you had to be very careful that the aerial did not get cut.

Courageous did not have the latest Action Information Organization, which was just appearing. The RN was rather slow to introduce computer-aided methods of solving the 'Bearings only' problem posed by detection of the target bearing only. It takes a high degree of detective work to solve the target's course, speed and range when the only certain information you have is a collection of bearing lines. *Courageous* did have DCD using the Ferranti computer. However, DCD could provide just about any solution you gave it as one of the variables had to be decided before you had a hope of solving the problem! Basically there was no substitute for the old fashioned methods of plotting and trying to fit in the best solution on the bearing lines drawn on a plotting table. Then trying to track your best solution on the Torpedo Control equipment.

One gadget we had as the result of a boffin's work at the Underwater Detection Establishment was a prototype active sonar intercept equipment which could give us a lot of information about active sonar transmissions helping to identify the source and range of the transmitter. We called this gadget 'Donald' after its inventor. Although it was only in the prototype stage it was a tremendous improvement on the old Type 197 intercept sonar equipment.

In order to fit us for our role in the 'Cold War' we carried out a lot of training in the Attack Teacher at the Clyde Submarine Base at Faslane. Whilst we endeavoured to put the lessons to good use at sea it is one of the facts of life that 'Worse things happen at sea!'

I must emphasize that the success of a submarine is the result of a team effort. In the case of an attack, the estimations of the target's course, speed and range will be made by the Captain. He will be aided by his observations and experience but the capability of the team, the tubes' crew, trimming Officer of the Watch and many others will have all contributed to the successful outcome. All the same factors applied to a Cold War patrol, and one should never forget the technicians that have been responsible for propelling the submarine, and ensuring that all the complex equipment works.

Training

The 'Fast Cruise' is not named because of any speed involved, but from the submarine being made 'fast' to the shore. This is an American expression. It has proved to be an excellent method of preparing a nuclear submarine for sea after a maintenance period or prolonged spell in harbour. Basically the Ship's Company live and work onboard the submarine, being firmly secured to the jetty, for a period of about two days. Every aspect of the submarine's operation can be safely exercised. The watch bill is proved to be effective and even the galley's effectiveness to cope with the requirements of the 'Two watch system' can be tested. Much of the machinery and operating procedures will be thoroughly examined and exercised. With a little imagination it is amazing how realistic life onboard can become in spite of not being actually at sea.

The crew was never a static entity after our workup. So we had a constant supply of new blood arriving and having to be trained up. This constant battle to maintain standards was an extra load on my hard working experts.

Operations at sea

Cold War operations required plenty of sea time. We had to practise trailing and surveillance operations and work in an integrated way with the Americans. I had a full briefing about the SOSUS organization, which was then a Top Secret 'need to know' subject. Nowadays it is freely talked about on the TV and is well documented in various books.

In order to achieve our tasks we developed a highly effective 'Two Watch System'. The object was to ensure that the submarine could undertake longish operations with the minimum of disruption. The Captain was one watch leader and the Executive Officer (usually known as the First Lieutenant) the other. If there was another Command qualified officer onboard he would be assigned the Captain's watch leader position thus releasing the Captain for overall control. The sonar, communications, plotting and ship control teams were split in two. Each watch lasted for six hours and people not required in slack periods could stand down. The propulsion department remained in three watches. Obviously much thought had to be given to the planning of meals and the timing of the watches. By the time I left we had a highly effective system in place and the submarine employed it whenever at sea. I believe that the system was widely adopted in the SSNs later on. An illustration of the system is placed at the end of this chapter.

It is of interest that my Coxswain, Brian Densley, was employed as a Ship Control Officer of the Watch. In the past this had always been a junior Officer's post. This novel arrangement worked well and I understand that it became an accepted position for experienced Senior Ratings later on in our submarines.

The Captain of a nuclear submarine has a fair amount to consider. He will become almost paranoid about 'Atmosphere Control'. There has to be just the right amount of oxygen, not too much, not too little. There must be no contamination of the submarine's atmosphere with unwanted gases such as freon from the cooling plants etc. The percentage of carbon dioxide in the air was always to be considered. The list always seemed endless. Life was made even more difficult by the electrolyser, which produced oxygen, interfering with our sonar. Therefore we had to resort to burning oxygen candles. The large numbers involved presented enormous stowage problems especially as used ones had to be retained until they could be ditched. Another major concern was the question of 'chlorides'. Contamination of the feed water system in a nuclear plant was akin to bubonic plague, as such impurities could do untold damage to the system.

Luck will always be a significant factor in life underwater. This is often forgotten, especially by anyone who claims things solely for himself. Murphy's Law has a habit of delivering a sharp reminder to those who are cocksure. 'What can go wrong will go wrong'. Therefore it is vital to have a well trained crew, confident in their ability, as well as the ability of their crewmates, so that the unexpected can be dealt with, as well as the day to day details of submarining. This was especially important if the 'Two Watch System' was to be effective. Incidentally, nothing annoys me more than non-submariner authors writing in ignorance of the glaring truths of all this!

The provision of films was an essential method of relaxation during the off watch time. The picture of my Navigating Officer emerging from the cabin which had the screen over the doorway one afternoon is a continual reminder of the film *Patton*. The cabin had been continually shelled for some time and he had a mild case of 'shell shock'! We played a number of games in addition to the usual card games. Uckers, the naval version of Ludo, was always being played. The rules were often in dispute! No submarine Captain liked to lose! When activity permitted a quiz night could be laid on. Light reading was the usual thing as it required little concentration.

The Cold War

It is common knowledge that American and British nuclear submarines carried out extensive surveillance operations against the Soviets. Unfortunately officialdom prevents any details of these activities being made public. The appearance of a book called *Blind*

HMS Courageous, *Author's birthday cartoon*

Man's Bluff was much heralded as a revelation of the 'untold story of Cold War submarine espionage'. Whilst it must have raised a few eyebrows when it was published much of the contents is given to speculation with little factual detail. This was inevitable because of the way the authors had to obtain their material. As a nuclear submariner, with some knowledge of the subject, I found the book difficult to read. In this country the official line is that only information which is already in the public domain can be freely published.

The Werm

One of the lasting features of the *Courageous* was the ship's newspaper, named after the snake that adorned the submarine's crest. It was a scurrilous newspaper illustrated by an expert

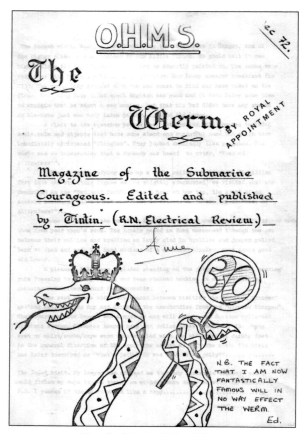

'Royal edition' of The Werm

cartoonist. I was often to be found in the contents! The first occasion was when a young Leading Stoker was told to 'shake the Captain'. He did just that as he had not been told that 'shake' was naval parlance for a wake up call. So I was shaken like a rabbit! The next occasion was when the periscope was very stiff to turn. I told the rating, detailed to be the periscope assistant, 'Push me'. He took this literally! Both these episodes are remembered by the crew some 30 years later!

Princess Anne, as she then was, came to visit and spend a day out at sea with us in the Clyde. She had just been had up for speeding. The Royal Edition of The Werm had a crowned snake clasping a 30 mph sign in its tail. It also showed a stubble-chinned Coxswain Densley as the stand-in in a flowered frock for the 'Rehearsal'. I am the proud possessor of a signed copy of this unique document! A photograph of Princess Anne looking through the periscope with me at her side appeared in the national press. My Captain SM, Martin Wemyss, referred to this as the beauty and the beast! Flag Officer submarines, Tony Troup, accompanied the princess, and he had a minor accident in the First Lieutenant's cabin when the wooden sink cover came crashing down on his nose when washing his face. It had not been secured properly. He was not in the best frame of mind when the First Lieutenant tried to present him with our specially prepared memento of the Royal Visit!

Events

The submarine's crew proved their prowess in the 3rd Squadron's sports and won the trophy and a splendid cake. They won four events out of the varied programme and proved that hard work is no hindrance to sporting activity.

The tradition of a *Courageous* garden party was kept up and we had a fine sunny day. Long white trousers did look slightly out of place in the Clyde but they do look smart as an essential contribution to 'garden party rig'.

Four of my young Lieutenants had splendid weddings during my time. So I went to equally enjoyable weddings in Scotland, London, Sussex and the New Forest.

Visits

The programme did not allow any exciting visits. We went to Haakonsvern with the NATO Standing Force. With Bergen as the only near town and previous experience of this part of Norway meant it was of little interest to me in our only foreign visit during my time in Command. The 'Thanksgiving Day Lunch' aboard the USS *Bigelow* was a grand affair. It remains a pity that American ships continue to be 'dry'.

As a bit of a joke we arranged a Home Port Visit with Stirling. Stirling is in the middle of Scotland virtually equidistant between the Faslane base and Edinburgh. It could hardly be described as a port. I switched on the Christmas lights with Miss Stirling and we had the Provost onboard, visiting his first nuclear submarine.

HMS Courageous, *Author's departure 1973*

I left *Courageous* astride a towed torpedo with some pride and lots of happy memories. I had handed her over to Andy Buchanan, confident that she would be in safe hands; after all he was a student of mine! Later I was fortunate to be awarded an OBE for the work that this fine submarine carried out. The OBE is always termed 'Other Bastard's Efforts'. Whilst this is a truism, someone should show off the reward for all their hard work, and I have always hoped that my crewmembers shared that view!

Tricia and I went to the re-dedication of *Courageous* in October 1986. It was to be her last commission. Nearly six years later in April 1992 we attended the 'paying off' of this splendid submarine. There was a dinner onboard the evening before for all the ex Commanding Officers. All ten of us attended at this unique occasion. In the visitor's book I wrote, 'Rust in Peace' but this was not to be as *Courageous* was to be reborn as a visitor attraction 10 years later. So we were invited to this rebirth in Devonport dockyard where she is now settled in dry dock and had a glass of bubbly to drink the health of the old lady after the opening ceremony. Once again we had a few survivors of the old *Courageous* present. Indeed, providing the money can be found the future looks bright. Much voluntary work has resulted in the resurrection of what had been a submarine destined to rot. My old RP2, Mr Pitkeathly, who likes to be known as Pitt K, has proved to be a mastermind in persuading people to get cracking. The guides are all volunteers and enjoy showing the public round the front section of the submarine. At present the opportunities for people to visit are limited and centre around Navy Days and those occasions that the Devonport naval museum is open to public view.

I am now the President of the *Courageous* Association, which meets periodically at different venues in the UK. This idea was put into practice by Chas Cooke who served in her in the latter half of the first commission. His enthusiasm was boundless and ensured that the Association got off to a great start. I must confess that it is a humbling experience to be greeted so warmly by members of one's old Ship's Company.

Illustration of the Two Watch System

	Captain	
Position	**1st Watch**	**2nd Watch**
Watch Leader	Captain or Command qualified rider if available	1st Lieutenant
Tactical OOW	TAS Officer	Communications Officer
Ship Control		
Ship Control OOW	Torpedo Officer	Coxswain
After Planes	Radio Electrical Artificer	Petty Officer Steward
Fore Planes	Leading Writer/AB	Leading Stores Assistant/AB
Systems Console	Mechanician	Mechanician
Systems Console Assistants	2 MEMs	2 MEMs
Tactical		
Torpedo Control Calculator (TCC)	Navigating Officer	Supply Officer
DCD	Electrical Officer	Chief Electrical Mechanician

TGCU	Chief Electrical Mechn.	Chief Electrical Mechn.
Local Operations Plot (LOP)	Leading Seaman RP	Leading Seaman RP
LOP Assistant	AB	AB
Contact Evaluation Plot (CEP)	AB	AB
Time Bearing Plot (TBP)	Petty Officer RP	Leading Seaman RP
TBP Assistant	AB	AB
Range Plot/Periscope Assistant	Electrical Mechanic	Leading Electrical Mechanic
Recorders	Leading Writer	Leading Stores Asst.
Sonar		
Controller	Petty Officer	Petty Officer
Passive	Leading Seaman	Petty Officer
Sector	Leading Seaman	Leading Seaman
Intercept/Underwater Telephone	AB	AB
Wireless		
Radio	Petty Officer	Petty Officer
Electronic Warfare		
Electronic Systems Intercept	Leading Radio Mech.	Leading Radio Op
Others		
Cooks	Petty Officer/Cook	Cook/Cook
Stewards	Steward	Steward
Messmen	AB	Steward

CHAPTER 17

Captain Submarine Sea Training

1973: CSST

I WAS SELECTED TO HEAD UP THE NEW Submarine Sea Training Organization. Flag Officer Submarines had been beset by a number of 'incidents' recently and decided to ensure that submarines were better trained, both at sea and in harbour. Since I had not been selected for promotion to Captain on the last list, then I would take up the post as an Acting Captain. It took a while for the wheels to turn, and meanwhile, I spent the time writing down my thoughts for Fleet Submarine Operations in order to update the various publications.

Eventually, sporting my fourth stripe, I moved to Faslane with the family to No. 3 Carnban Road. This was not a Captain's quarter, but the original Commander's House. We did not mind, as the appointment was to be relatively short, as I was to be a stand-in until Sandy Woodward was available to relieve me. I do not think that he was the right choice. In his book he did say that perhaps he smiled too little and hatchetted too much, and he had not had the experience of being a Commander SM under a splendid Captain SM. If he had, he would have taken a more sympathetic attitude to the training problems posed to his organization.

I was again lucky to have a very experienced collection of Officers as well as Ratings to get this new organization off the ground. It had a very broad compass of responsibilities. Harbour Training prior to workup post building and refit, the COs' qualifying course, FASMAT (the nuclear reactor training simulator) and the Command Team Trainer. The prime task was the working up of submarines after their refit or on completion of building. In the case of Polaris submarines only the safety workup was included in my responsibility and not the Operational workup, as this remained the responsibility of their Squadron Commander, Captain SM 10th Squadron. Later on the submarines that had had extended

Sea Training Staff

134

maintenance periods were to have a shortened workup to get them ready for operations again.

Initially this was too large an organization and later had to be slimmed down. Once the first teething problems had been overcome the responsibility for the CO's course reverted to the Captain SM of the Third Squadron.

Hugo White was my Commander Sea Training. He was a most professional and gifted Officer. He did become an Admiral and in my view he should have been First Sea Lord. When I left this job I told him to make his way in General Service and get out of the Submarine Stream, which he did with great success! Unfortunately when he was an Admiral his wife became very ill and he was forced to resign in order to look after her.

The seagoing staff and I spent quite a bit of time going out in the submarines either for a day or longer and sometimes hopping from one submarine to another out in the distant sea areas by helicopter. This kind of transfer once resulted in a trip round HMS *Warspite*'s fin on the end of the hoist wire but below the level of the fin and not too far off the surface of the sea! All in all it was a busy time but very satisfying. It was a welcome task to visit submarines in refit and breathe a little salt air into their atmosphere.

It is a difficult to strike the right balance between training and judging the capability of those that have to respond to that training. If one is too critical they become disheartened. If the highest standards are not insisted upon you are neglecting your charges. I suppose it is the old problem of stick and carrot but one has to be adept in judging when to apply the appropriate requirement. I think it is best if the Staff adheres to seeking the best and leaving it to the Captain to play the part of the bluff old codger who understands their problems. I would not pretend that there is any easy solution, as every now and again you will be forced to give a kick up the backside.

So eventually I was promoted legally and after a total of only nine months I handed over to Sandy Woodward. Not for the first time, as he had relieved me as Teacher of the COs' Course back in 1967, seven years before.

CHAPTER 18

The Ministry of Defence

1973–74: ADNW(P)

THE MOD IS OFTEN CALLED THE Madhouse. It was and still is! The joke department installed me as Assistant Director Naval Warfare (Polaris), ADNW(P) for short. I knew nothing whatsoever about Polaris. I had the honour of working for three Admirals: David Scott as Chief of the Polaris Executive, Peter Berger as Assistant Chief of Naval Staff (Policy) and Admiral Branson as Assistant Chief of Naval Staff (Operations).

Much of my work was Top Secret, especially as it concerned Polaris and its updating. This was the Chevaline project and it figured very highly in day to day business for many months. It was really a continuation of an American project which they had abandoned in favour of the Poseidon missile and then Trident. The highly theoretical requirement arose because it was thought that the Russians could defend Moscow by shooting down incoming nuclear warheads, thus nullifying the UK's deterrent. It was obviously very popular with our scientists, as it would be a great flag-waver! All projects greatly exceed the cost estimates quoted to Ministers. Chevaline was no exception, and it certainly cost at least three times the first agreed cost. Whilst all this is now water under the bridge with the Cold War ended and Trident firmly in place as the National Deterrent I do hope that the full story will eventually be told, as it would be a case study in how not to embark on a project.

I could call on assistance from two Commanders, Paddy O'Riordan and Ian Pirnie, both of whom became Admirals. Paddy was more concerned with general submarine matters whilst Ian was the Polaris weapons expert. It was a delight to work for David Scott and Peter Berger. I did not have a lot to do with Ops. Nuclear reactor safety was naturally very important and when any problems arose I had to brief Peter Berger, especially when it affected the Deterrent. There was a splendid occasion when the only nuclear qualified Engineer in the whole of the Main Building was not consulted when the First Sea Lord, the Controller and the Director of Naval Warfare met to discuss a reactor question. Such are the oddities of the Naval Staff system! Admirals seldom dealt with the lower echelons and some Officers were far too proud to call upon an expert.

Much time at the Ministry was spent writing copious 'papers', many of which were to support some project or other. Usually the weaker the case the more paper was to be expended. Two such projects readily spring to mind. One was the acquisition of a naval manned tug for Faslane in case of strikes and a Diving Ship for the Royal Navy. Both of these projects cost a lot of sweat and much money with no real gain and both were discarded pretty soon after being taken into service.

I never quite worked out why the amount of time spent in an office in the Main Building determined the success of one's job. Henry Leach, who was a brilliant Officer and the ACNS(P) before Peter Berger, used to be in his office well before the Staff officers arrived and he met them on the doorstep as he went out for breakfast. Many an Admiral was conducting business well after 6 p.m.! No Director of a Division would want to be found wanting so they stayed until all hours. Many people had no family home to go back to, only a cold small London flat awaited them, hence the lack of urge to live a civilized life. I commuted to my home in Bucks. It was of course financially very attractive to live on Lodging Allowance in London and just see the family at weekends, but what a way to live.

I have never understood the apologists who make their name in the MoD saying with great conviction – 'we fought against these defence cuts but however vigorously we fought we still lost'. Personally I applaud those who resign rather than let the political steamroller flatten their ideals. Some of these apologists believe the pen is mightier than the sword. Unfortunately those who have to fight require swords! The paper warfare of the MoD was something I loathed and I was very glad to never have another appointment there! I think that the biggest problem in the MoD was the many-layered organization that then existed. Generally speaking, it is a great disadvantage to carry the 'one over one' type of

MOD, Polaris Executive, Author with 'Lunchtime Garters'

organization to its ultimate conclusion of everything being bogged down in one of the layers.

I managed a trip to Iran. This was for a CENTO meeting. I went because the desk Officer who should have gone was unwilling and I thought it would be an unusual experience. CENTO was then showing all the signs of being something that had no real purpose. I remember that I had to make a presentation about an obscure piece of equipment that could be fitted to a frigate to assist jack stay transfer. The chap who should have been talking about it had little knowledge of the thing and certainly I had none. My presentation to a completely uninterested audience was a disaster.

The meeting was in a naval base in the north of the country. Driving was not a pastime that attracted the highest intelligence in Iran. An Italian officer was nearly killed one night when the car he was in left the road! I was in a car on the way back to Teheran which was forced to leave the main road when a shambling lorry just pulled out from the side in front of us. We were going quite fast and I believe the car was unusable after we came to a stop. It was certainly an alarming experience!

The following definitions were acquired during my stint at the MoD. I do not remember where they came from but they exemplify what the seagoing naval officer thought about this lunatic asylum!

An expert	is a man whom you think will confirm something you want to believe is true
A menace	is the expert who doesn't confirm something you want to believe is true
A poor chap	is an expert whom avoids confirming or denying something you want to believe is true
A good chap	is a man who feels the same way about experts as you do
A nice chap	is man you do not understand but is polite and cleverer than you are and avoids asking experts
A bloody man	is someone who isn't there
Winning	the art of believing others are losing
Losing	discovering your expert is a menace
Delicately balanced	losing
Equal honours	losing
Technocrat	anyone with O level Maths
Scientist	someone with more experts than you
Buddy	a white foreigner

CHAPTER 19

Captain SM Tenth Submarine Squadron

June 1976 to May 1978

THE JOKE DEPARTMENT CONTINUED WITH THEIR previous success and made me Captain in charge of the Polaris Squadron. Apart from the first ones, which included John Fieldhouse, all the others had commanded Polaris Submarines before and after me! So I was to be an exception! The family moved back to Carnban Road and only a short distance from where we resided during my Sea Training Days. This job also had the additional title of Queen's Harbour Master Clyde so there was another learning experience.

The Polaris School, complete with its leaking flat roof, was also one of my responsibilities. Why is it that we cannot build a place with a flat roof that does not ultimately leak like a sieve? I was also to get acquainted with the Armament depot at Coulport where the missiles were stored, serviced and loaded onto the submarines.

I went out in the submarines for their pre-patrol periods and missile training, and the workup of *Resolution* including her DASO firing at Cape Canaveral in 1977. It was quite an experience to be onboard a Polaris submarine firing a missile albeit, and thankfully, only a practice one which was fully instrumented. The visit to the USA gave me the opportunity to see the Space Centre and stand on top of the Vehicle Assembly Building. This building is so high that clouds form inside it. Also I made the obligatory trip to Disney World to sample the delights of 'Space Mountain'!

Looking back, I was invited, together with my wife, to a large number of social functions, many dinners, cocktail parties, paying off parties etc. It was nice to have a Wren driver and car at my disposal. I did make one mistake when I drove myself to the Mudhook Yacht Club annual dinner. This august body does not actually have a clubhouse as such and was founded many years ago with a finite number of members plus one forbye, who was drunk and under the table when the club was formed! Champagne is

HMS Resolution, *Polaris missile firing 1977*

served throughout the meal and is passed in carafes, which have a round bottom, between the diners. These carafes are priceless so it would be a hanging offence to drop one! I should not have driven myself there! So I did not drink as much champagne as I would have liked.

One day I spent a night onboard the USS *Hunley*, the US depot ship at Dunoon for their SSBNs. At breakfast next morning there was a gleaming white tablecloth in the Commodore's mess where the COs of the submarines also ate. By one plate there was a galaxy of pills, presumably every known vitamin and then some. I have always alluded to this as the technicolour breakfast. It was not long after that I witnessed an American officer pouring a generous helping of maple syrup over his fried egg at breakfast in the officers' mess at Cape Canaveral. Everyone to their own taste but the Americans do not regard breakfast in the hallowed way that we do!

One dinner I especially remember was the 75th Anniversary of the Submarine Service at HMS *Cochrane*, the shore base at Rosyth. I sat next door to Sir Francis Peto Bart. He had been the Captain of A12 in 1915–16. He also served as Captain of the M class submarine fitted with the large gun turret in the 1920s (M2). He was a most interesting man. I learnt later that he had had two silver weddings having married his wife's sister after his first wife died. Having retired from the Royal Navy in 1931 he had the rank of Honorary Commander. He had his blood changed once a month due to a blood problem and lived in solitary state near Ayr, although by then well over 80 years of age. He drove himself to Rosyth and had never been on a motorway before, hence his surprise to be driving on the M8! He invited me to come and stay with him so I could record his memories for posterity, and laid on a special little dinner for me with his pals. He was then aged 88!

One of the most important events as far as I was concerned was the Silver Jubilee Fleet Review. Tricia and I had a grandstand view of the Royal Yacht as she left Portsmouth harbour to go round the fleet escorted by HMS *Newcastle*, which was gleamingly smart. The dinner onboard HMS *Ark Royal* that night was a great occasion. All the Captains of the assembled ships were present, as were the Squadron Commanders. It was with some pride that I could say that three quarters of my Squadron were at sea on this occasion, the other submarine being in refit! Each of the diners received a commemorative plate as they left *Ark Royal*.

The journey to and from the outer Londonderry areas by Sea King helicopter was very very boring so I decided to read a book on the way. I selected *Watership Down*, as it was a very interesting story and a nice fat paperback. Unfortunately the weather for disembarkation from the *Resolution* was pretty rough and as I stood up to my waist in surging water at the base of the fin it was decided to do a fin transfer to the helicopter. *Watership Down* had been flooded and all the pages stuck together so no reading on the way home. Tricia painstakingly dried out every page for me!

The Polaris submarine patrol was subsequently fully analysed by the PPAG, the Polaris Performance Analysis Group (now called the

Resolution Class Polaris submarine

Strategic Performance Analysis Group). The analysis determined whether there had been any detection by Soviet forces, and the actual readiness of the Polaris weapon system to fire. Dummy firing procedural messages were sent during the patrol to keep people on their toes, and to ensure the effectiveness of the deterrent. It was customary for a submarine returning from patrol to be met by an Admiral, or senior Politician whom I accompanied. The Captain of the Submarine then gave a debrief of his patrol. It should never be forgotten that such a patrol required navigational skills and sonar skills of the highest order, as well as the normal technical expertise required to ensure that everything kept running.

We gave a number of dinner parties, but one of the best was later known as the 'Power Cut Supper'. In the winter of 1978 snow lay deep in the Loch Lomond valley and brought down the power lines that supplied the Base. Just as the guests were due to arrive the lights went out! Fortunately the house was warm and the food almost ready. The would-be hot chicken dish was hastily converted into an interesting orange salad dish. Those guests who managed to make it

Dining out Admiral Troup

through the snow came bearing candles, and a good time was had by us all. The only mishap in the dim light was somebody poured mayonnaise onto their pudding thinking it was cream! Two days later there was still no power in our electricity dependent house and we got frozen. Therefore we were forced to evacuate to the wardroom for a while.

One of my tasks that developed because I was relatively senior was to give farewell speeches at wardroom guest night dinners. I prefer to do this without notes so I used to learn my lines just like an actor. One particularly enjoyable one was that which I gave for the departing Commander. As the Wembley Horse Show was only recently over I compared his time at Faslane to a number of jumps! I also had to say farewell to Spiv Leahy, who had been a very successful Commodore of the Base. He was an ex-flier so we submariners got on well with him.

Dinner parties in the wardroom of a submarine are very special and as the Polaris submarine wardroom is so very large they are indeed very special. Admiral Tony Troup, when retiring from his post as Flag Officer Scotland, was dined onboard *Renown* with Flag Officer Submarines, John Fieldhouse, as host. Admiral Troup was a most distinguished submariner who had terrified quite a few submariners during his various appointments as he did not suffer fools gladly!

My departure from the post of Captain SM was quite a day. A suitably dressed crew of my staff officers rowed me aboard a whaler to *Resolution*. Onboard *Resolution* I was welcomed with a glass of champagne with their crew turned out to greet me. From there I travelled in a very decorated pickup truck complete with band in the rear to the wardroom for a farewell drink.

So ended my active naval career with the Submarine Service. They were the best of days in my naval career and occupied most of it!

Fortunately my submarine career had spanned the whole gamut of modernization, and progressed from the introduction of the snort,

Author leaving 10th Submarine Squadron 1978

more batteries and higher voltage electrics to allow higher speeds from the electric motors and finally nuclear propulsion. Weapons had progressed from the well tried Mk 8 torpedo, which had always been required to run straight to being angled, thus allowing the submarine to operate in a less limited manner and not necessarily having to be pointing at its target. The requirement to be able to attack submerged submarines saw the progression of the electrically driven torpedo which could 'home' on its target, to those which could be wire guided to the target and actually ping on the target in the final attack mode. Sonar developed from whites of the eyes detection ranges, to vast long-range detection with the advent of towed arrays and advanced signal processing. Satellite communication had changed the whole concept of the control of a submarine from Head Quarters. Likewise satellite navigation permitted precise navigation and the ability to fire submarine launched missiles. Navigation had also been enhanced by the Submarine Inertial Navigation System (SINS).

The complexity of a modern submarine requires much more professional knowledge than hitherto. As more and more advanced equipment is carried onboard there is more and more emphasis on equipment reliability, as modern electronics do not easily permit the 'fix it' attitude of yesteryear. Nor do nuclear reactors allow patching up as we used to with reluctant diesel engines!

CHAPTER 20

HMS *Fife* – In Command

December 1978 to October 1979

AFTER A LARGE NUMBER OF COs' Designate Courses based at HMS *Dryad* near Portsmouth I eventually joined my one and only surface ship command. *Fife* was a lovely looking ship armed with: Sea Slug, a much outdated anti-aircraft missile; Exocet in a mounting forr'd in place of one of the original gun turrets, a modern anti surface ship weapon system; Seacat, a short-range anti aircraft missile system, which was not very effective; and the remaining 4.5-inch gun turret. She had two gas turbines as well as the normal boiler and steam turbine arrangement. So she could go quite fast but burnt fuel as if it was freely available. She had a Type 184 sonar, and a Wessex helicopter (affectionately called Humphrey) that was also getting outdated, for use in the anti-submarine role. With a Ship's company of 450 with 33 officers there was plenty to occupy the mind.

I took over rather late in the Commission from Jeremy Black, later to Command the *Invincible* in the Falklands campaign and destined for high rank. There was no chance that I could change anything significant so I did not even try. I had a sneaking suspicion that the sonar team would be unable to detect a submarine unless they could see it! They had certainly not received much training or experience in anti-submarine matters.

My first fuelling attempt on the way to Gibraltar was a waste of time; it was far too rough and called off before we even got into position. The second attempt was rather harrowing as *Fife* would just not steer properly and we had to do an emergency breakaway. It was only when divers revealed that one of the two rudders was severely 'moth-eaten' that it became clear why I had had a problem. We spent the next few days in Gib getting repaired in dry dock. This meant that we missed our sea inspection by our Flag Officer although we did get to fire a Sea Slug very successfully during Exercise 'Spring Train'. Whilst *Fife* was being repaired, Ian Grant,

HMS Fife, *damaged rudder 1979*

who was Chief of Staff to Flag Officer Gibraltar, put me up and entertained me right royally.

Our next scheduled trip to Gib was cut short when a Russian Task Force, with their Carrier *Minsk*, passed close by on their way to the Far East. This was a pity as Tricia had come out to Gib for a few days. So *Fife* was scrambled without our helicopter, as it was defective, and chased after the Russians making a grand sight creaming out of the breakwater at high speed. Quite what was achieved I do not know. It was a very successful exercise in assembling a scattered Ship's Company prior to sailing at very short notice. We did take some lovely photographs as we tailed them for a while. It could not be for long as we were due to visit Lisbon and this southerly course was taking us in the wrong direction.

Ship's Company HMS Fife *1979*

Lisbon was great fun. It is a very interesting place with tons of history. The Portuguese Navy provided me with a car and driver. As I was very interested in the Peninsular war, the British Senior Naval Officer on the NATO Staff put me in touch with a retired Chartered Accountant who had studied the subject. He directed my driver to Torres Vedras as well as the remains of some of the fortifications of the Lines. I also had a lovely relaxed Sunday afternoon, with my Commanders, drinking Madeira in the grandest hotel in Lisbon, a throwback to Edwardian days.

On return to the UK we were duty ship and then sent off chasing a Soviet *Kresta* class destroyer. We picked him up eventually at night in the Minches, and later chased north with him until we had to turn back because of fuel requirements. Unfortunately we were again without our Wessex for probing contacts. The *Kresta* was obviously working with a submarine and made sure that we could not see whatever device he streamed. We were some 400 yards astern of him when he enveloped himself with smoke from

Hunting the Kresta: *stern view of a Soviet* Kresta 2 *from* Fife *bridge*

prearranged smoke floats so we had to withdraw a bit for safety reasons. Later, I annoyed him by crossing ahead of him on his way north and intercepted his underwater telephone conversation with the suspected submarine.

After an exercise we visited Hull. This was a great success. I had the honour of judging Miss Romeo and Juliet at the nightclub of that name. The manager was extremely hospitable to us all. Escorting the Royal Yacht from Portsmouth to the Clyde for the Queen Mother's visit followed the Hull visit. The Duke of Fife was embarked in *Fife* and presented me with a splendid case of vintage port. I gave half of it to the wardroom and kept the rest for personal consumption. I drank the last bottle at home many years later and wrote and told the Duke of this event. I had a nice letter in return advising of the vastly inflated price that particular vintage now enjoyed. We have never drunk something so expensive!

It was an amusing experience to take my ship into Faslane. We berthed ahead of the Royal Yacht (naturally without tugs) and over the harbour intercom came the message to remember that HMS *Resolution*, which was just ahead of my berth, had a stern that stuck

HMS Fife, *sails past Royal Yacht, saluting the Queen Mother, off Arran*

out underwater. Perhaps they had forgotten who was commanding *Fife*, and it made everyone smile on my bridge!

Dinner on board *Britannia* that evening was a splendid occasion. I sat on the Queen Mother's left hand and the Duke at her right. The next day we steamed past the Royal Yacht and cheered Her Majesty. We did indeed look smart as the photographs taken from the Britannia showed. We berthed at Hunterston on the other side of the jetty to the Royal Yacht almost at the same time! After witnessing the formal opening of the ore terminal at Hunterston we left for our visit to Aarhus in Denmark. I believe Hunterston was another example of wasting public money for political gain.

The next port of call after Aarhus was to be Cardiff where we flew the Flag of Peter Berger, then Flag Officer Plymouth. Cardiff made us very welcome. I much enjoyed visiting the old coal exchange which had been a very busy place in years now long past. It was now merely a comfortable club. Cardiff docks were deserted save for one Russian ship. The Cardiff Docks Board gave us a very expensive lunch to which we were driven in very sleek 4.5 litre

Jaguars. As the Docks Board was at that stage broke I found it all a bit surprising!

The next item on the agenda was Exercise Highwood, a NATO exercise with a scenario of the Russians starting the conflict at sea. All rather pointless as the result is obvious to me. He who hits first has the advantage! I often wonder whether exercise planners are real!

Now off to the USA — via Bermuda, for a short stop. I bought Tricia a bottle of perfume there and asked the assistant the price. She asked 'how much is your wife worth sir?' Next stop was Cape Canaveral and Tricia joined me on arrival. It was fun to take a destroyer into this traditional submarine port. There were lots of parties, as the Americans were as hospitable as ever, the record being three in one day. A visit to the Kennedy Space Centre and the Assembly building and, of course, Disney World so my wife could see these great attractions for herself.

Thence to the Bahamas to Freeport. Jack Hayward the millionaire looked after us all right royally. He paid for a night out for many of the Ship's Company. He is very pro British and enjoys proving it with his support. I had a splendid time playing golf at the Lucaya Country Club. As it was August and off-season (too hot!) we had the course to ourselves, and golf buggies had been provided too.

After a shore bombardment exercise on the US range at an island near Puerto Rico, we visited San Juan. The rain forest at the eastern end of the island was spectacular. San Juan is filled with history. The Dorado golf course set amongst lovely trees was a place of great beauty and calm. Once again the Ship's volunteer band gave a splendid display of 'Beating Retreat' at the ship's cocktail party. They had already done this at Cape Canaveral and Freeport so they were becoming quite expert. They brought a lump to the throat. The Americans were most impressed, as they do not have anything to match such a display.

Then off to Tortola in the British Virgin Islands. I called on the Governor by helicopter using our Wessex. Then rejoined the ship as we anchored the other side of the island for a banyan on the beach for the Ship's Company next day!

I have decided that I am now enamoured with the ways of the surface world. They are so different from that which we Clyde veterans experienced! This is rather like taking a holiday at Butlins after a spell in Dartmoor!

Next stop Antigua. I had not been here since I was a cadet in the HMS *Devonshire*. Nelson's Dockyard is now a significant attraction and much souped up. The Cedar valley golf club was rather bare and unexciting as well as expensive as we had to pay for our buggy.

It was nice to win a bottle of Remy Martin from RFA *Cherry Leaf*, our accompanying tanker for fuelling astern, a complicated manoeuvre, with a total dead time of 17 minutes. It is certainly a convoluted way of getting fuel when compared to our normal abeam method.

Homeward bound when a hurricane struck the island of Dominica, so we were diverted to render assistance to this devastated island. Hurricane 'David' swept through the island on 29 August 1979. As we approached next morning it was not difficult to see the destruction in the capital, Roseau. We could not get alongside until the next day because of the heavy seas but we employed the helicopter to render First Aid to the hospital and to land my Commander, John Wright, to establish the exact state of affairs. I wrote a long report about our assistance to Dominica and a precis of this is included as an Appendix (page 156). As a result of this operation the Commander was awarded an OBE, three officers including the helicopter pilot got the MBE and three ratings gained the BEM, including my Chief Cook who ran the airport so well. The ship was awarded the Wilkinson Sword of Peace. A number of Officers and ratings were given a commendation by the C-in-C Fleet. The Helicopter crew also won the Boyd Trophy. All of us were proud to have contributed to this relief operation and here is the message sent to the Queen by the President of the Commonwealth of Dominica.

On behalf of the people of the Commonwealth of Dominica I wish to express our deepest appreciation of the invaluable assistance which Captain Fry and his crew of HMS Fife *rendered to our stricken country after the devastation caused by Hurricane David. They arrived on our shores at the darkest hour and lit the first beacon of hope. Their relief efforts were ceaseless and untiring. Their devotion to duty a shining example of their friendship in our hour of need. Captain Fry, Commander Wright, the helicopter crew and the other commanders and members of this gallant crew exemplified the highest traditions of the British Navy. On behalf of myself as well as on behalf of*

HMS Fife *returns to Portsmouth 1979*

the Government and People of Dominica I wish to express the thanks and eternal gratitude of this nation.
Signed Jenner Bourne Maudee Armour President
of the Commonwealth of Dominica

We had a nice relaxed passage home and arrived back at Portsmouth a bit later than expected. Chief of Staff to C–in–C Fleet, Admiral Staveley, and Keith Speed, the Navy Minister, came out to meet us by helicopter. So I berthed alongside HMS *Kent* for the last drive in Command and rather unexpectedly my wife and daughter were right opposite the bridge on board *Kent* to greet me.

We had lots of nice messages awaiting us and once Customs had been cleared I hurried home.

I must confess now that my seagoing time in command was at an end that I agreed wholeheartedly with Admiral Hezlet, who said when he was Captain (D) of a destroyer flotilla, 'Always take a pilot even if you only say good morning and goodbye'. Some of them seem to be hell bent on disaster of one sort or another!

Fife was now to take on a new role as Fleet Training Ship for New Entry ratings direct from the New Entry training establishment at HMS *Raleigh*, so that they could experience shipboard conditions, albeit safely alongside in harbour! The idea was to bridge the gap between shore training and a billet at sea by giving them a taste of things to come. As this was a completely new venture we had to be inventive and a lot of thought went into planning the curriculum for the brand new chaps in the ways of the sea in spite of being harbour bound!

During my last few weeks with *Fife* my wife and I attended the White Ensign Association Banquet at the Great Hall in the London Guildhall. We were put up that night at the Savoy hotel and this gave us an avid taste for the high life. Tea being served in our bedroom on a pink tablecloth with the most delicious cakes ever is mouth-watering memory, even today!

Later on I was also invited to a Variety Club lunch at the Savoy. Now I was off to a new appointment as Chief Staff Officer Reserves to the Commander in Chief Naval Home Command, to whom I had been responsible for starting off the Fleet Training Ship.

I took this job in preference to being Chief of Staff to Flag Officer Submarines, which I had been offered. A staff job, miles from the sea, after all my happy years closely involved with salt water, had little to commend it. The prospect of 'holding the fort' at HQ whilst my Admiral enjoyed travelling around the parish filled me with gloom! It may well have harmed any promotion prospects, as I was now destined for a non mainstream appointment, but this was of little consequence. Therefore life at Northwood was not an attractive proposition, even though it would have been within commutable distance of our home in Chesham Bois. I remember being asked by my appointer at one stage in my career whether I was ambitious. I do not have any great feeling for ambition, so I said 'Not particularly'. I have often wondered what the purpose was of this question! He could have asked whether I wanted to be happy doing a job to the best of my ability and then he would have got a detailed answer.

HMS *Fife* hurricane relief operation

30 August to 5 September 1979

*F*IFE WAS ON HER WAY HOME from the West Indies when she was diverted to go to the assistance of the Island of Dominica which was struck by Hurricane David. It was decided to arrive off the island at first light sending in advance parties by helicopter, the first requirement being to establish the first aid actions required. The advance party consisting of the Commander, a Warfare Officer and a Communication rating found a chaotic situation on arriving at Government House and persuaded the Prime Minister to establish the seat of Government at the Police HQ. The Deputy Marine and Weapons Engineer Officers and the Medical Officer then strengthened the advance party.

Hurricane David, damage to hospital in Dominica

30 August

The ship had to wait offshore as the sea was choppy and the wind blowing Force 7. It was apparent that we would not be able to berth alongside until the next day. The devastation of the capital, Roseau, was plain to see from half a mile to seaward.

Personnel were transferred to the Hospital that had been effectively blitzed. It needed major reconstruction, re-roofing, and resurrection of some ward accommodation as well as the operating theatre. Medical supplies, blankets and water were supplied during the day. The Commander set off in the helicopter with the Chief of Police and the Medical Officer for a reconnaissance of the areas most in need of assistance. By the end of the first day a clearer picture emerged of the damage, and those areas where the ship could usefully give aid. The main priorities for working parties were established as water supply restoration, road clearance to the airfield, and hospital repair.

31 August

On the next day, 31 August, it was planned to send in nine helicopter sorties to progress the main tasks. The ship refuelled from RFA *Cherry Leaf* before going alongside Banana wharf having had to wait for a coaster to vacate the berth. Once the ship was alongside at 1245 the major effort was applied to the restoration of the hospital with the helicopter going here there and everywhere with drugs, medical stores, personnel and casualty transportation. I called upon the President, visited the Police HQ and the ruined hospital, where the ship's team, under Lieutenant Lippiett, were making magnificent progress.

1 September

The third day, Saturday 1 September, was the day of maximum effort in the three priority areas. During the afternoon I went to see how the road clearance operation was going, Apart from the large remaining landslip the situation looked much more hopeful.

This morning Radio Dominica had been established in the Operations Room and we were broadcasting pop music and government announcements. The Prime Minister came along at 5 p.m. to make a long broadcast to his people. During the day a number of ratings started street clearance in the capital, with the aim of inspiring the local people to do something for themselves.

2 September

On the following day it was clear that consideration would have to be given to when, and how, the ship would be disengaged from relief operations. The Ship's Company was now displaying signs of both mental and physical exhaustion. Hurricane Frederic now threatened and this gave the right moment to haul off for a while, and go to Barbados where two Hercules aircraft were scheduled to land with stores from the UK.

The working parties ashore had been most successful. The road to the airport on the other side of the island was now open to traffic. Sufficient work had been done on the water supply to allow the flow to the capital on the next day. The hospital was becoming

Hurricane David, blockage of road to airport, Dominica

shipshape by the hour. We slipped that evening and arrived at
Barbados next morning. We learnt that the two Hercules had not
yet started to unload to the lorries scheduled to take the stores to
the ship. I did not think much of the initiative of the two RAF
Captains. I thought they lacked a sense of priority in an emergency
situation.

3 September

In spite of this delay the Ship's Company soon loaded some 40 tons
of stores. A further 15 tons of stores from the SS *Sun Francis* were
embarked also food supplies purchased by the British High
Commission. The ship sailed soon after 6 p.m. The hangar was full
and stores lay everywhere!

4 September

We arrived back at Dominica at 7 a.m. next morning, Tuesday 4
September. A large party was despatched to the hospital.
Unfortunately although water had flowed to the capital, Roseau, on
the previous day, the supply had silted up, so another party was
dispatched to the dam to fix things.

During the night a flash flood had occurred at Melville Hall
airport. Buildings had been flooded and stores damaged. Large
throngs of locals were milling around in a near riot and there had
been looting of relief supplies. At the request of the Dominican
authorities the helicopter took a mixture of ten armed police and
local defence force to the airfield, and order was soon restored.

By now a French tented camp was discovered. It was all neat and
tidy with tricolour flying. Having established their advanced field
hospital their single project was road clearance to Grand Bay. Aloof
and Gallic, they did not appear to want to acknowledge our
presence!

After a tour of the town and a visit to the US water purification
unit, which was now producing 800 gallons of fresh water per hour
from the river, I went to see Radio Dominica. This local radio
station was now back in operation although the building
exemplified 'Dominican disease'. This is the ability to sit with chaos
all around and do nothing about it! Thence to the hospital where

the rehabilitation of wards and re-roofing were proceeding apace. Lastly to the Police HQ to confer with the Commander. It was decided to have a Council of War on board at 6.30 p.m.

Following Humphrey's last flight today (Humphrey was the Wessex helicopter), vintage champagne awaited members of the aircrew and the Ship's flight. Humphrey had now achieved five days of dawn to dusk flying; this must have been some sort of a record for an ageing Wessex helicopter. The flight deck crew was joined by the President of Dominica who wished to thank the aircrew personally for their efforts. He later toured a selection of messes to give his personal thanks and then had supper in the wardroom. At the Council of War I recounted the ship's activities to date. Then I gave a gentle prod to the Prime Minister and the various aid authorities represented at the meeting to make them realize the need to start planning properly. As an example I was concerned about the administration of the hospital after we left. After the meeting I realized that our helicopter would be required next day as no other helicopter was available to distribute food to inaccessible areas.

5 September

After landing our liaison team, still headed by the Commander, *Fife* slipped from Banana wharf and patrolled offshore. SS *Geest Star* then moved alongside and unloaded her supplies from St Lucia. Three small coasters later berthed alongside to add their cargoes to the island's stocks.

I decided to withdraw this evening on completion of helicopter operations for the day. Indeed the Wessex had airlifted 17,500 pounds of food. So after re-embarking the liaison team course was set for home.

The experience of this relief operation was and will be proudly remembered by all onboard. I believe that at that time Royal Navy Ships were the only ones carrying Hurricane Relief stores whilst visiting the Caribbean.

Postscript

Following the report of *Fife*'s operations Flag Officer Sea Training introduced realistic disaster relief training for ships undergoing workup. In addition a film called 'The Unexpected' was made as a result of our experiences and was to be used for training.

In my report I had a section about International Disaster Relief. I think that the statements I made are as true today as they were then.

Until actually involved in a disaster operation, the average naval officer will be totally unaware of the inefficient manner in which relief activity is conducted. Not only will the titles of people and their organizations be unfamiliar but also the amount of 'clout' they possess will be difficult to assess. Experience in Dominica clearly points to the advantages that accrue from early personal contact at all levels with the throng of people that will appear, from the US State Department man, down to the lowliest Red Cross representative.

All will wish to communicate with their boss/agency. All will have different priorities. All seemingly will be more wrong than right. Yet out of the chaos order will somehow manifest itself. If the ship has the only worthwhile outside communications, at least the cables and messages can be seen. It is vital to 'censor' these communications, albeit in a tactful manner, so that the more outrageous and misleading statements do not add to the confusion. For example, several days after the disaster the Red Cross representatives were about to send a communication to their HQ, which contained glaring errors, gross exaggerations and demonstrably ill co-ordinated ideas.

It would be ideal to have a Daily Planning Meeting with all these various people but time is too short and priorities are rather more on the crisis management level than those arrived at in the good order of a ship's organization. In any case, politically it would be disastrous to assume that one can overcome prejudice, national characteristics and world political considerations even during a disaster. So a compromise will be arrived at, more by accident than design. Initially the ship is well placed to lead people in the right direction. There is certainly a distinct possibility that given the right circumstances the ship can become the quiet, relaxed pivot of an operation, and thus aid the achievement of cool, calm and wise decisions. Furthermore, it will be easier to grasp what all the individuals hope to achieve and how they are endeavouring to carry out their plans.

CHAPTER 21

Chief Staff Officer (Reserves) – The RNR

1980–1983

M Y FINAL JOB IN THE ROYAL NAVY turned out to be with the Royal Naval Reserves (RNR). I had hoped that someone would have acted on the recommendation from my service in HMS *Fife* for another sea command but these things are decided in some place divorced from reality. I had a happy time with the RNR with my longest appointment ever in one job. The Royal Navy appeared to know little about them. I certainly knew absolutely nothing. The RNR did not appear to be too troubled by this so perhaps both organizations were too inward looking to acknowledge the other!

The extent of my responsibility was vast. There were 11 Sea Training Centres (STCs). They were at London, Southampton, Shoreham, Newcastle, Edinburgh, Dundee, Glasgow, Liverpool, Bristol, Cardiff and Belfast. The STCs had to provide a crew for their allocated Minesweeper or Minehunter. They also had to provide up to two other crews to meet their wartime requirement. The RNR's ships formed a Mine Countermeasures Squadron under the command of a RN Commander with a small staff. Plans were afoot to re-equip the RNR with a trawler type vessel fitted out for deep-armed team sweeping of deep-laid Soviet anti-submarine mines. There were other branches of the RNR attached to the STCs such as doctors, dentists, chaplains, supply etc.

There were also 11 Communication Training Centres (CTCs). They were mainly in the centre of the country at Exeter, Nottingham, Birmingham, Manchester, Preston, Stockton, Sheffield, Leeds, Southend, Swansea and Coventry. Their task was to provide Communication ratings, both men and women. They had a senior RN rating permanently attached to the unit, which was usually situated near the city centre. Other branches could have members attached to the CTC so that the recruiting base was able to accommodate a variety of specializations.

The remaining major units were the Head Quarters Units at Portsmouth, Plymouth, Northwood, Chatham, Rosyth, Greenock and Gibraltar. Their task was to provide support to the local area Commander mainly with plotting and communications.

There were a number of other valuable yet small branches within the RNR. There were a number of outposts such as the postal branch at Mill Hill, Intelligence at Ashford, Naval Control of Shipping in the Channel Isles and Milford Haven and, later on, the Air Branch at Yeovilton.

The RNR's intelligence branch had a number of sub branches, Photographic Interpreters at RAF Wyton, Interrogators at Ashford (later to be HMS *Ferret*) and Linguists who were particularly valuable.

The Naval Control of Shipping was an arcane science, which the Royal Navy had not kept up since World War II. The RNR had kept it going for many years with ageing officers, mainly administered by the Officers' Mobilization section of the Naval Secretary's Department. After my time it was recognized that the RNR needed to recruit and train new blood to ensure that the task could be met in the future.

With such a widely spread and diverse organization I had to do a lot of travelling as I had to see the ground, meet the people and listen to their concerns as well as spread the gospel! My small staff of specialists did likewise. To give some idea of my itinerary I made 37 trips in my first year and 38 in the second. This eased a bit towards the end, just 33, and then 13 in my final 4 months! I attended numerous dinners, as the units were most hospitable and generous. I also went to Bisley every year to see them shoot. It was good to see that the RNR kept up an interest in using small arms. The RN seemed to have given up what used to be termed 'Land Fighting'. There was a feeling that a sailor with a gun was a menace to his own side.

My first major date was the Commissioning of the RNR's Air Branch at Yeovilton. The RNR's Air Branch has been a major success story having survived many defence cuts since. It marked an interesting development that has spread to other specializations. The

Author visiting RNR Unit in Gibraltar

creation of a hybrid between the Regular and the Voluntary
Reserves by taking only ex-Regulars, and keeping them up-to-date
with some training as Volunteers rather than leaving them to
moulder on a Regular Reserve List. In the past these ex-Regular
Reservists had become steadily out of date and therefore quite
useless!

A major matter that had to be addressed was the future of the
List 1 Merchant Navy Officers. Historically this had been the
original Royal Naval Reserve and still consisted only of professional
Merchant Service Officers. The number of these Officers, within
the then RNR, was declining due to the internationalization of
shipping and the consequent reduction in British merchant service
manpower. The requirements of the Navy for these officers had also
changed with the advances being made in naval warfare.

Traditionally List 1 was an entirely separate entity from the rest
of the RNR and even had its own naval training rules. A previous
Commodore List 1, John Wacher, had been tasked to address this
issue but his report and conclusions needed updating.

Tony Barrett was the Captain RNR in List 1 given this task and
the broad outcome of his investigation was twofold. Firstly that List

1 should become more integrated into the general RNR. Secondly, that the specific skills and strengths of professional seafarers in List 1 should be aligned to existing Naval requirements.

He visited many Naval operational and training organizations and found particularly fertile ground with the newly appointed Commodore Amphibious Warfare. The Commodore had considerable concerns about his ability to lift and deliver the substantial logistical support by the Commando Brigade for the potential deployment to the flanks of the NATO Alliance.

Early in 1982 Tony Barrett was assigned to the annual North Norway Amphibious exercise on Commodore Amphibious Warfare's staff. This resulted in the appreciation that List 1 Officers had a natural and highly valuable role to play as liaison officers on board the merchant ships taken up from trade (STUFT). These were required to carry out the logistical lift for the amphibious forces. Another spin-off was that Commodore AW's staff could now appreciate that merchant ships were deployable within a naval force and could be relied upon to respond professionally to operational requirements.

This exercise had taken place in February 1982. It was indeed fortunate as just two months later, in April, the Task Force was assembled for Operation Corporate to retake the Falkland Islands. It is noteworthy that Commodore AW went on record saying that the one concern he *did not have* was the ability of the ships taken up from trade to be fully integrated into his force. Whilst the timing of Captain Barrett's work was fortuitous it was an excellent example that the RNR had much to offer if only the RN could recognize it!

There is now an established role of amphibious warfare specialists within the RNR. Another aspect of these investigations was the identification of a requirement by Flag Officer Submarines for trained headquarters staff in 'water space management'. This role is now an established task for RNR Officers.

The remainder of the RNR, and the major portion, were on List 3. They also had their own Commodore. I was concerned that there appeared to be only one route to Commodore List 3 via the Captain's appointment to the RNR's sea training billet. Furthermore the RNR appeared to give no thought to future policy. Therefore I created a new post, Captain Plans and Policy for

Captain John Wightman, the then CO of the STC at Edinburgh, HMS *Claverhouse*. This also ensured that I could get him to be the next Commodore List 3 if required. This proved to be a very worthwhile and happy selection. Indeed John became Commodore in due course.

One of the problems with the RNR at this time was the absence of 'war appointments' for many of them. I tried to establish some wartime rationale for them in the Royal Navy. However, I met with little assistance as the RN was singularly ignorant of what the RNR could offer. It was only when the RNR was cut in half at the end of the Cold War (as well as the eternal wish of politicians to spend as little as possible on the Armed Forces) that some attention was given to this particular requirement. John Wightman and his Assistant, Superintendent Wendy Peters WRNR, was tasked with this essential work of modernizing the HQ Branch. This resulted in the 'HQ Report'. The major change recommended was that HQ Officers and ratings conformed to the specializations of the RNR. The HQ units were a guarantee that the RNR could not be axed. They worked directly for Admirals, who could not man their HQs for exercises, much less go to war without them. This was not widely understood! John used to say that I tossed the grenades into the fray when it came to policy and he was then sent in to sort it all out!

I was always impressed by the keen attitude adopted by the RNR in spite of the rather standoffishness approach of the RN. Many of them had responsible jobs in civilian life yet they were prepared to give up their spare (and very valuable) time to the RNR. This involved many hours during the week and their annual training period. In addition many activities occurred at weekends like the RNR Boards, Bisley, etc.

I was the President of the Boards for junior RNR officers wishing to qualify for their watchkeeping certificate. The other members of this Board were senior RNR Officers of various specializations. This was another weekend activity.

I was invited to a cluster of dinners as the RNR had their own events to celebrate as well as the traditional Trafalgar night dinners. Terence Cuneo, the famous artist, always attended the postal branch dinner at Mill Hill, which was in an Army mess there. The mess had some of his paintings on display.

Both Tricia and I were invited to dine formally in the grand cabin of HMS *Victory* by the C-in-C on two occasions. This must be the highlight of anyone wishing to dine in the naval environment. History is all around and makes a lasting and vivid impression! We also attended a grand occasion onboard the *Victory* as guests of a White Ensign Association celebration. We dined on the gundeck with a plank table suspended near a gunport. The very place where the 'sons of guns' were born. All the assembled guests were issued with a ship's biscuit, but there were no weevils! The meal was served by suitably dressed 'powder monkeys'.

There were many important RNR events. The inauguration of the RNR Air Branch at Yeovilton in 1980 set the ball rolling. The reopening of HMS *Cambria*'s STC at Barry after moving from dilapidated quarters in Cardiff in October of that year was a noteworthy occasion as this was one of the RNR's prime units, being the home unit of Bob Hastie, then Commodore List 3. In 1983 I officially opened the new premises of the Nottingham CTC.

Bob Hastie was a most successful Commodore and it was a pleasure to work with him, although his driving around Lisbon after our trip with the RNR's minesweepers was a little nerve wracking! He knew his way around the RN and the Ministry and was not afraid to let people know his views.

Following the integration of the former List 1 RNR Officers with their training regularized and common with the remainder of the RNR there is now a single Commodore RNR. Indeed as events have moved on the Commodore has more of a functional role rather than the advisory one had during my time.

Every year the COs of all the RNR units met with the Commander in Chief, the Reserves Division Staff and the Commodores. The Communication Branch, Electrical Branch and Engineering Branch Officers had periodical meetings held at the appropriate RN School.

It was through the good offices of John Wightman that I had a round of golf at Muirfield. My golf was not up to the standard necessary but it was a course to remember. The bunkers at Muirfield reminded me of my inauspicious visit to one at Dundee when playing with a particularly dour Scot. I played the hole quite well by my standards having covered over 400 yards in two shots but

Author receiving Wilkinson Sword of Peace, awarded to HMS Fife *following their assistance during Hurricane David*

unfortunately I was in a greenside bunker. I took nine shots to get out and was in fits of laughter towards the end and the Scot got more and more dour!

There were occasions when my time in HMS *Fife* connected with the hurricane relief operation resulted in further engagements. Princess Margaret invited me to Kensington palace. I attended the presentation of the Wilkinson Sword of Peace, which was presented to me on behalf of *Fife*, by the then Admiral of the Fleet Sir Terence Lewin. I also went to HMS *Osprey* at Portland to see the Boyd Trophy presented to my old ship's flight, which they had won because of their sterling work in Dominica.

I had a loose connection with the Sea Cadets as CSO(R) and visited a few units. Later I became the president of the local unit in Chesham. I was particularly asked to visit the Epsom sea cadets where there was a very lively unit.

There were opportunities to visit the Channel Islands to acquaint me with the Naval Control of Shipping contingent there as well as those at Milford Haven.

Boyd Trophy presentation to Humphrey's aircrew

In October 1981 we had a term reunion for those of our Dartmouth term who had joined in January 1944. It was held at HMS *Mercury* and most of the term was discovered although some were never found. Alas the term failed to produce an Admiral but we did produce a circuit judge. It was surprising what a diverse collection of jobs everyone found after leaving the Royal Navy.

1983 saw a round of farewell dinners and parties. The RNR Communication Branch presented me with a magnum of Vintage Port. This was consumed some 21 years later at Christmas time and it was delicious! The RNR Senior Officers dined me at *Claverhouse* in April and presented me with a mini tape recorder and a splendid replica submarine badge made of brass. This was found in an antique shop and it is so large that we often wonder where it originated.

In July 1983 I retired from the Royal Navy.

Post Script

All these years later the RNR reflects the major cuts that have been inflicted on the Royal Navy in the post Cold War period. Much of what was achieved during my time as CSO(R) was negated. That is progress! There have been the customary frequent reviews which are to be expected in the piping days of peace, especially when money is tight. Nevertheless I was proud to see the RNR still going relatively strong when Tricia and I attended the Centenary parade on Horse Guards in May 2003. Prince Charles presented the Sovereign's Colour to the RNR in recognition of their 100 years of service. The march past was particularly impressive. They did not march so smartly in my day! I hope that they will now enjoy a period of stability and perhaps regain some of the lost ground. Units have been disbanded in centres of population where the RNR was the sole naval presence. This is more than a pity.

CHAPTER 22

Retirement

1983

O BVIOUSLY AFTER WEARING UNIFORM for over 39 years the immersion into civilian life is a bit of a shock! I had a choice of doing a 'Business Acquaintance Course'. This is held in London in the City and informs a mixed audience about business, particularly the financial side, with a game about production, cash flow etc. The course would probably benefit the younger person but it was not very relevant at my stage of life.

Now I was faced with seeking a job. I had a CV prepared but I think that when you are in your 50s the CV is of little interest to someone who is actually after a younger person. I got two interviews quite quickly: one to be the Secretary for SSAFA, the other to be Secretary to the RAC Club. Having got on the short list for both of these I had a decision to make. The RAC had a lot of attractions with responsibility for the Golf Course at Epsom; the Old Crocks race to Brighton, Derby Week, and not least the Club itself in London. Unfortunately I would have to wait some time before a decision was to be made. Then an opportunity came up to work for Marconi Underwater Systems at Wembley, which was to be well paid, provided a car and use my naval experience. It had the main advantage of being within driveable distance of our home in Chesham Bois and was available immediately.

So I chose Marconi. It was almost certainly the wrong decision but that is the wisdom of hindsight. My task was to lead a team to make a computer simulation of the submarine attack. It sounded most interesting! However, as it turned out no one there really knew what kind of simulation was required or how it was to be achieved. Efforts were made to get Ferranti and Plessey involved but in the end they showed little or no interest and as it turned out they were to lose their independence too.

The final outcome was a project named by me as COSMOS (Combat Submarine Overall Simulation). It was to be all singing all

171

dancing with the ability to slot in pieces of software such as a Spearfish simulation or indeed a Stingray simulation. The management was persuaded to buy a very expensive parallel-processing computer for our new establishment at Croxley Green together with a secure environment which would enable top secret work to be simulated with no chance of electronic surveillance. It all cost a lot of money. The Duke and Duchess of York duly opened the magnificent building at Croxley Green. We gave a splendid presentation of our colossus to the GEC Board, including Lord Weinstock.

No one at the MoD was at all interested in our endeavours and eventually both my technical expert and I were made redundant. We were not the first to depart from Croxley by any means, as Marconi was not selling anything really. If the truth were known the writing was on the wall with the end of the Cold War by 1987. The Defence Industry was about to catch a cold!

So there I was high and dry at the end of 1987 looking for a job that would pay sufficient to enjoy life. We had thought of moving to Dorset to be near Tricia's mother who lived in Charmouth. Then I discovered that Lyme Regis Golf Club was advertising for a Secretary. This was something I had considered so it was a tremendous surprise and very welcome. I survived my first interview and was invited back for a second. After this I was pressed that evening to make a decision so that was how I arrived at Lyme Regis Golf Club as their part time secretary for the next seven years.

Lyme Regis was just modernizing their administration and had acquired a computer and the software from Club Systems to put the membership details into a database and allow invoicing to be achieved in a modern manner. One of the members, General Peter Benson, assisted me in this task as it does take some time to put well over 600 people's details into the database.

I had a lot to learn about golf clubs and the way they worked as well as handling the competition results etc. The new computer system allowed for automatic adjustments of handicaps and printouts of competition results. It must have been quite a task before all these modern methods of presentation and solution!

Much time at Golf Clubs is taken up with Committees. This club had just changed to the modern system of a Management Committee and a Captain's Committee. The latter now only concerned itself

Lyme Regis Golf Club centenary 1993

with golfing matters whilst the Management controlled the Finance and Course as well as the Clubhouse, Bar and Catering. There were thus a minimum of two evening Committee meetings a month. I was to find that my part time job extended to six days a week, which included Sunday. Usually only from 7 a.m. to 1 p.m., but sometimes later! There were a number of weekend competitions, which I had to run on Saturdays during the spring and summer. Additionally I might actually get to play golf myself in some home and away fixtures. So I was busy but usually enjoyed it all, particularly the Open Day competitions when I bought the prizes and had to arrange the tee off times, opponents etc. They were something that I could call my own!

An excessive amount of time was spent deciding whether to have a new clubhouse or modernize the existing one. The General Meetings whether Emergency or Annual seemed to generate a lot of heat, but eventually we arrived at a nice modernized clubhouse, which although never ideal, was visually pleasant, and provided most of the facilities required by a good golf club. During the build my office was in a portakabin in the car park! I was greatly relieved when all had been completed.

One of my victories was to get the accounts on to the computer. By now I had a very able assistant and after a trial run we learnt sufficient to get it all up and running for the new Treasurer to accept this modern way of accounting.

I was most touched by being given a retirement dinner with Tricia. We were given an engraved decanter, glasses and tray, a bottle of malt whisky, even a camellia plant from the Ladies Section. Now aged 65 I could count myself as fully retired.

CHAPTER 23

Finale

I HAVE ARRIVED AT THE END OF MY MEMOIRS. I have enjoyed the task and I hope that the reader will have obtained some enjoyment too. I do not know who said it originally but the saying 'All the problems of the world are those of Communication, by thought, word and deed' has always figured in my life. We could all spend more time 'communicating'.

Whilst I have been happy with the writing of all these words I have been beset by computers which consign text to cyber space at the drop of a hat. It seems very difficult to communicate with today's computers!

It is traditional for the author to thank all those who helped create his work. I therefore am indebted to those former members of *Courageous* who encouraged me to write down details of my career. Naturally I also need to highlight my wife's part in all the proceedings as it is now our Golden Wedding year, so she has suffered 50 years! She has recently been censor, proof reader and suggestion maker!

I finish with a quotation that I have frequently used and endeavoured to follow:

'If the trumpet give an uncertain sound, who shall prepare himself for battle!'

Domestics in the Navy

I HAVE USED THIS TITLE for a separate section of these ramblings because they may not interest everyone, so anyone who likes can skip them.

I was issued with a naval paybook on becoming a cadet at Dartmouth, so this historic document dates back to January 1944 and is now falling apart. In 1951, as a newly promoted Lieutenant my pay was 17s 6d a day, that is 87½p in today's money, and to this was added submarine pay of 4s (20p). Submarine pay was a significant sum! My pay increased to 21s 6d in November 1952 and by the time I was 25 and married with the full marriage allowance I was getting £1000 a year.

The paybook was used to record vaccinations and inoculations as well as travel warrants issued. It also records such fascinating details as 129 clothing coupons issued in July 1947 for the purchase of tropical clothing as rationing was still in force. There was also a space to record Medical examinations called PULHEEMS. The table shows a distressing increase in weight from 170 lbs to 195 lbs in 19 years! as well as deterioration in my eyesight. Squeezed in are details of chest X-rays as these were an important part of submarine fitness for obvious reasons. Also there are details of Submarine Escape Training completed once the 100 ft escape tower was in use. It was a periodic requirement to requalify at frequent intervals in order to continue to receive submarine pay.

Throughout my naval career I was never really able to say I was exactly rich but we never really wanted for anything substantial and things were purchased according to the priority at the time.

Gieves was then the naval tailor and providing you made some attempt to pay off the amount owing all sorts of things could be purchased on credit, and there was no credit charge then. So although Gieves gave you a taste for good quality their continued support to the Royal Navy allowed naval officers to enjoy much that would have been denied in civilian life then.

Payday, at the end of the month, was always eagerly awaited, as we did tend to live on a knife-edge. As an example, our joint account recorded a credit balance of just over £2 early in our married life.

One of the greatest benefits we enjoyed was an educational allowance, which gave us the ability to send our children to boarding school when it became necessary. This gave them a valuable and very necessary continuity of education, as we did move around a lot. Our eldest son clocked up eight different schools by the time he was eight! The allowance did not cover all the fees by any means but it let us stomach the fees that then existed. As a proportion of income the fees were far less than today – thank goodness. Our eldest son David joined the Navy, and we had the pleasure of going to his passing out at Dartmouth as well as to the City University in London when he got his degree. Strange to see a naval officer in uniform wearing a gown and mortarboard! The other son did a gap year with the Ghurkas as an Army engineer before going to Oxford. He did a short course at Sandhurst and we went to see his passing out ceremony there. The Army is so well organized that they put up the fathers the night before the passing out parade and entertained them to dinner with their sons and the staff. I was particularly impressed by the non-commissioned officers. Whilst at Oxford he changed to the RAF and joined the ATC there. He was soon flying solo and bent on a pilot's career. Once again to a passing out parade but this time at Cranwell. We told a RAF officer on the staff that we had been to all three Service Colleges for their passing out ceremonies!

Both our sons later changed career but our daughter stuck to hers. After qualifying at Amersham Arts College she became a graphic designer working for two advertising agencies, the latter specializing in theatre work. Then she became self employed and has worked on a variety of different projects. All the packaging for the Covent Garden Soup Company and their soup books are samples of her talents. Lately she has been working for Green and Black and their Chocolate Book was another labour of love. All the children are now happily married and we have some grandchildren to carry on the family name, so we think we have done our bit!

We have always believed that hobbies should play an important part in one's life. One hobby at the very least should be outdoors and one indoors. We have spent many happy hours making toys for the children and grandchildren. The list seems endless, recently some 110 hours were spent refurbishing a much loved but dilapidated early 1900s dolls house. Furniture restoration can keep anyone very busy and my pride and joy is the dental cabinet which had been painted white. It has been restored to its former burr walnut glory! Once you get hooked nothing will deter you from a task and I now have a miniature Waterloo army of some 3000 figures, all painted with a mixture of oils, enamels and acrylics. I have painted quite a few of the larger figures but they are really time-consuming! Tricia has always been busy making things, clothes, curtains, cushions as well as the usual doll's outfits. Working with wood is much easier than fabrics! Outdoor activity is easy whilst young as there are plenty of sports to amuse and ensure that you mix freely with different people. Golf can be a lifetime's interest but latterly the garden has taken over most daylight hours.

Over the years we have developed an abiding love of gardening. This is not surprising as we have developed no less that five gardens from scratch and lovingly restored much of a cottage garden. Even our caravan site in Bute had a garden. Two of our new gardens were for Married Quarters as we were the first occupants. This always presents problems for a sea-goer as time to garden is a scarce commodity and gardens, especially in their early months, require lots of attention. New plants and newly established grass grown from seed always need watering. Whilst cash was always a problem we were also inhibited by the likelihood of having to move out at some unknown time in the future. The new garden in Malta quickly established itself as geraniums grew like weeds although water was a scarce commodity for watering plants there. Two of our gardens have been for the two new houses that we have bought during our life. The first was in Buckinghamshire at Chesham Bois and was eventually extended from its original small plot by purchasing a piece of land from the Abbeyfield House at our rear. This allowed us to have a larger lawned area, a second shed and even a sandpit for the children. The second, and we hope, our last new garden is in Dorset at the lovely village of Whitchurch Canonicorum. There is a comfortably sized plot, which gives unfailing pleasure as well as lots of work! During the last 17 years everything has grown up so

Author's garden in Dorset 2005

much that the garden now looks very mature. We have over 200 perennials and shrubs, 20 roses, 30 conifers and a few trees. There is a useful vegetable plot and a valuable fruit cage.

The cottage garden that we helped to restore was situated at a pretty thatched cottage in Lacock in Wiltshire. It belonged to a schoolmaster at Westminster School and was used as a holiday home for his family down in the summer holidays. So we had to move out then. The garden had been lovely but was now somewhat neglected because of the part time occupancy. Loving care and the radiant roses meant that people would often stop at the front gate to admire this Old World charm. Our book entitled 'Gardening from Scratch' will probably never be written, but it has been fun gaining the experience.

Jottings

The Americans

WITHOUT EXCEPTION I HAVE ALWAYS found the Americans most generous and hospitable. Their naval officers are well trained but I have never understood their preoccupation with seaman officers having to be expert engineers as well. The RN has been fortunate in keeping its dividing line of technical excellence with the professional engineers.

I remember the Captain of the USS *Ethan Allen* proudly telling me that every stores note passed through his IN tray. A ballistic missile submarine is reputed to have as many different stores requirements as an aircraft carrier with squadrons embarked (so I have been told!). Therefore it seems ludicrous to me that the Captain should concern himself with such unimportant details.

Perhaps it is this almost Germanic concentration on details that irritates me most, as there have been many brilliant US submarine COs who have been able to dispense with this limitation. I do, however, remember being amazed by the CO who proudly announced that he had had only two weeks leave in three years! Is this devotion required to get promoted?

The US Navy has consistently been able to give its submarines the best equipment. Their sonar kit far excels that of the British and their expertise with SOSUS meant that they enjoyed a head start in the use of towed arrays by their submarines, enabling them to detect submarines at long range and safely track them. The US Navy has had all sorts of other expensive and up-to-date kit well in advance of anything we had in our submarines, but it must not be forgotten that from time to time our scientists, with far fewer resources and much less cash, did pretty well. We must never isolate ourselves from the US.

American civilians have always been so hospitable that it has been embarrassing! They have gone out of their way to make me feel at home. The interest and warmth of feeling really hits you. In *Fife* our volunteer band doing their evening colours ceremony could bring tears of pride as they entranced our American guests.

The French

My first meeting with the French Navy was during my final year at Dartmouth. By then we were back at the college having returned from our wartime home at Eaton Hall at Chester. We were invited to the French equivalent of our training Cruiser which was visiting Dartmouth. We were plied with most excellent red wine and were very very happy when we got back to our stern monastic life! My next meeting was as a midshipman in the Far East when we visited the FS *Dougay Trouin*, an old French cruiser, where we were royally entertained by the enseignes, called aspirants.

As a Sub Lieutenant I had two French pen friends and also having joined the Linguist's club in Portsmouth remembered escorting two lovely young French girls round HMS *Victory*, when I tried valiantly to tell them lots of Nelsonian facts in fractured French. My French was rusty in the extreme having abandoned it as a subject of study in favour of Russian at Dartmouth.

When I was the Captain of HMS *Acheron* we were host ship to the French submarine *Narval*. She was brand new then and equivalent to our Porpoise class. She was also first of class. The CO was justifiably very proud of his submarine including the 'brushed' stainless steel everywhere (ordinary stainless steel reflected the light). He personally showed my wife round when we had dinner onboard. *Narval* was brilliantly prepared and we had a multi-course meal with the appropriate wines for each course. The only disaster as far as we were concerned was the liqueur served with the coffee, Mirabelle, a plum liqueur, which tastes quite disgusting! They very kindly sent over a bottle next day and it was ceremoniously poured down the sink just outside the wardroom!

The *Acheron* officers took the French officers out for a treat one evening to a pub on the Hamble which specialized in odd wines. I do not know what the French thought about birch wine etc. It was somewhat later in life that I realized that the French could be perverse. I went to a NATO meeting in Algiers where the French

Admiral and staff insisted on speaking French throughout in spite of all of them being able to speak fluent English. The Admiral had been with the Free French Forces during the Second World War.

Then again when I was commanding the Polaris submarine squadron a very senior French admiral visited and when we gave the Clyde Submarine Base presentation there had to be a simultaneous translation through earphones for him in spite of his fluency in English. He even asked questions in English!

It was at L'Orient that one realized the effects of Vichy France *vis à vis* the Free French. At a large French cocktail party there was just one officer wearing the Croix de Lorraine (the Free French badge) on his uniform and he was being studiously ostracized by his fellow officers.

I do not know the exact date that the exchange rate for a bottle of whisky changed from two bottles of champagne to just one! It was at Lorient that I was invited to a splendid lunch by a French naval officer and his wife. I gathered that his brother had been implicated in a plot against de Gaulle and had been shot! I have often wondered whether this was true.

The Turks

Having been to sea with the Turkish submarines on three occasions I had a great deal of admiration for the Turkish people. They were very friendly and hospitable. Their sense of humour is very similar to ours. They delighted in teaching me lots and lots of very rude words. They had an adolescent regard for sex. A Turkish submarine CO had invited his lady companion from the night's activity in Malta's 'red light' district, Strait Street, to come onboard his submarine next day. She appeared onboard. What a sight. Clearly no spring chicken, rather raddled with a vivid slash of lipstick. The Turkish First Lieutenant gave me a nudge, saying 'Night time is best time'!

The Spanish

The Spanish have always been hospitable and it was a great pity that they developed paranoia about Gibraltar. Having experienced the days when the border was freely open it was disastrously childish to close it for many years. They alienated the Gibraltarians quite unnecessarily, making it unlikely that there could ever be any agreement about sovereignty issues in the future.

The Yugoslavs

I only met up with their Navy at the Joint Tactical School in Malta whilst lecturing them about submarine operations. I have a limited knowledge of Serbo-Croat and with some help prepared my visual aids with Serbo-Croat headings and descriptions. I do not think I should have bothered as they were a very cold fish audience and gave no inkling of any interest in my spiel whatsoever. I think they must have all been Serbs, as I am sure that the other residents of that stricken country were livelier.

The Norwegians

I think that their navy tries hard with little funding. They have always maintained a small force of 'coastal' submarines and have kept up their contacts in the UK. The climate in their base at Haakonsvern is rather drab and it is miles from the nearest town, Bergen. They also have a drawback of not being allowed to drive after drinking just a small amount of alcohol. Drinking and driving attracts a jail sentence and people use their weekends to serve their sentence, referred to as being on holiday!

The Dutch

In many ways the Dutch are similar to the British, particularly in their Navy. We have always enjoyed particular co-operation. In the past we have trained their submarine COs, often having their candidate attached to a British course. Their expertise in NATO was always to be admired. They were a worthy adversary in their anti-submarine encounters during various exercises.

Golf

THERE WAS A SMALL NINE-HOLE golf course at Eaton Hall. Cadets could play on it once they had reached their senior terms. Consequently I wanted to play. I was left-handed with a cricket bat and there were few left-handed clubs available especially as the war was barely over. Therefore I would have to make do with right-handed ones!

I found my heart's desire in a pawnbroker's shop in Portsmouth. I got 16 wooden shafted clubs, called Hickory clubs, with a bag for £2! The next step was to find a course to play on so that I could get some practice in before having to demonstrate my non-existent skill at Eaton Hall. I phoned up Waterlooville Golf Club, which then was only a 9-hole course and later expanded to 12 holes. Mrs Payne was the stewardess and took me under her wing. She provided me with some golf balls; they were like gold dust then and cost 3s 3d each (16p in today's money). She took me out on the course to thrash around and eventually I had some lessons with the Pro, Mr Daish. He was a very friendly and hardworking man. In those days there were no green keepers and the Pro did absolutely everything.

In order to get a handicap whilst we were at Eaton Hall it was necessary to play the 9 holes in under 50 strokes. On one of my attempts I was going great guns having done the first 7 holes in some 35 shots. The only trouble was I took 10 on the eighth and 13 on the ninth!

Eventually I had a few lessons at Portsmouth Municipal Golf Course where the Pro, George West, was an excellent teacher. Lessons cost 2s 6d; this was a lot of money to me then! One day when cycling to Waterlooville with my clubs on my shoulder I was stopped by a policeman in the open country that then existed between Havant and Waterlooville. He wanted to inspect my bag as he suspected I was a poacher using the golf bag to hide my gun!

It is strange to think that in 1946 and 1947 I could watch golf at Brighton following the players in the News Chronicle Tournament along the fairways. I tagged along behind Bobby Locke and Dai Rees quite happily and you could hear them chatting to each other. Bobby Locke said once that putting on the greens was like putting on a coconut mat!

The Daily Telegraph Pro Am was held at Hayling Island one year. This is a difficult course to play at the best of times yet the experts made it look pretty easy including holing out from a very deep greenside bunker.

Serving Officers got a discounted green fee which helped to play courses which would have been too expensive for us or even denied to non-members. Eventually I became a member at Rowlands Castle but my service overseas meant I had to resign after a couple of years. The membership fee then was only 7 guineas. As a cadet in the Training Cruiser I played at a quaint little course at Bantry Bay with a young Irish lad as caddy. I wonder what he thought of our golf.

The course at Rothesay was great fun to play. There was one short hole where an errant drive went into someone's private property guarded by a fierce dog and an equally fierce Scotsman. However, golf balls were a valuable commodity then and needs must, so we often clambered over the barbed wire to recover our wayward balls, keeping a sharp lookout though!

My father in law was a very keen golfer. He had even played on the morning of his wedding day! His club was the Royal Richmond. They had a very fine Georgian house as their clubhouse. Ladies were not allowed in the Bar. It was a very friendly place and all the members knew each other on their Sunday outings. What better way to spend the day than 18 holes in the morning, steak and kidney pie for lunch after a few drinks, a further 9 holes and then a few frames of snooker before heading home.

I had the locker in *Courageous'* Captain's cabin suitably modified to take my set of golf clubs but that was a bit of a waste as we never visited anywhere during my time. I have always enjoyed playing alone if there was no chance of having a playing partner. This had a drawback when playing on a strange course as it was not very easy to know where the next tee was. I made the mistake of following a pair one day only to find that they were trying to avoid me and had their own particular way of playing the course for a 9-hole outing. They were quite annoyed with this idiot following them like an eager terrier!

Like most golfers I have lost a lot of balls but not all of them from bad shots! On the Downs near Bath the fairway was a field of daisies and I spent ages trying to find my white ball nestling somewhere amongst the flowers without success. I had the same problem on one frosty morning when the entire fairway was white! Nowadays you can purchase yellow or orange coloured balls, which show up wonderfully well.

In Singapore, in 1967 to 1969, I often played in Johore where there was a polo pitch inside the course. Woe betide you if you sliced onto the pitch if the sultan's son was playing polo. There was a bit of a difficulty there when the storms came as it was very open and the chance of being struck by lightning was very much increased. I always kept quiet about our odd rainstorms!

My golf has always been like the curate's egg as I have only really played intermittently over the years so the good shots are to be remembered and the bad ones hastily forgotten. Nevertheless, I would have regretted it forever if I had not played this frustrating but wonderful game. I am pleased to say that eventually I did get a 'hole in one' at Lyme Regis on the short 11th hole in winter with a No. 5 wood.

Glossary

AA	Anti–Aircraft (as in Guns)
AB	Able Seaman
ACNS(O)	Assistant Chief of Naval Staff (Operations)
ACNS(P)	Assistant Chief of Naval Staff (Policy)
ADNW(P)	Assistant Director Naval Warfare (Polaris)
ATC	Air Training Corps
AWOL	Absent Without Leave
Bird Bath	A canvas bath positioned under the conning tower to catch sea water and prevent it flooding the control room
CB	Companion of the Bath
CBE	Commander British Empire
CBNS	Commander British Navy Staff (Washington)
CENTO	Central Treaty Organization
CEP	Contact Evaluation Plot, originally all contacts plotted with bearing and time with additional qualifying information.
CinC	Commander in Chief
CO	Commanding Officer
COQC	Commanding Officers' Qualifying Course for Submarine Officers
CPO	Chief Petty Officer
CSO(R)	Chief Staff Officer (Reserves)
CSTs	Contractor's Sea Trials
CTC	Communication Training Centre for RNR
CV	Curriculum Vitae – a brief employment record etc
CVO	Commander Royal Victorian Order
DASO	Demonstration and Shake Down Operation, the firing of a practice Polaris Missile at Cape Canaveral

DCD	An early computer assisted method of target motion analysis
DSEA	Davis Escape Apparatus. Designed for Submarine escape using a small cylinder of oxygen
DSC	Distinguished Service Cross
DSO	Distinguished Service Order
ECP	Emergency Conning Position
Elephant's Trunk	A canvas cylinder positioned below the conning tower to catch sea water usually used in conjunction with the Bird Bath
ERA	Engine Room Artificer (a senior Engineering rating)
FOB	Forward Observer Bombardment
GBE	Knight Grand Cross of the British Empire
GCB	Knight Grand Cross of the Bath
GCIE	Knight Grand Commander Order of the Indian Empire
GCSI	Knight Grand Commander of the Star of India
GCVO	Knight Grand Cross Royal Victorian Order
GDP	Gun Directing Platform
Guns – A and B	Turrets or Guns – the forward mountings
Guns – X and Y	Turrets or Guns – the after mountings
HQ	Head Quarters, particularly applied to RNR units working for Area Commanders
HTP	High Test Peroxide – hydrogen peroxide propellant used for submarines and torpedoes
KBE	Knight Commander British Empire
KCB	Knight Commander of the Bath
KG	Knight of the Garter
LCM	Landing Craft Medium
LORAN	A Radio navigational position finding system
LST	Landing Ship Tank
LS	Leading Seaman
MBE	Member of the British Empire
MEM	Marine Engineering Mechanic (formerly a Stoker)

MoD	Ministry of Defence
MFV	Motor Fishing Vessel – used by RN as a harbour craft to transport stores and personnel to and from shore
MVO	Member Royal Victorian Order later changed to LVO
NATO	North Atlantic Treaty Organization
OBE	Officer of the British Empire
OECD	Organization for Economic Co-operation and Development
OM	Order of Merit
OOW	Officer of the Watch
PC	Privy Councillor
PO	Petty Officer
RAF	Royal Air Force
RAT	Rothesay Attack Teacher
RD	Reserve Decoration
RNC	Royal Naval College (Dartmouth) evacuated Eaton Hall during WW 2
RNR	Royal Naval Reserve
RP	Radar Plot rating: a number indicates seniority, 1 being the most senior and more highly trained
SBA	Sick Berth Attendant (later changed to Medical Technician)
SBS	Special Boat Section (Royal Marines)
SEATO	South East Asia Treaty Organization
SM	Submarines, indicative of Specialization or Title, e.g. Captain or Commander SM in a Submarine Squadron.
Sonar	Types indicated by number e.g. Type 186. Usually the higher the number the more modern the type. The newest sonars have 2000 numbers e.g. Type 2001 in first generation British Nuclear Submarines
SOO	Staff Officer Operations
SOSUS	Sonar System Under the Sea, an American seabed very long range sonar detection

	system developed to detect Soviet submarines in the Atlantic and Pacific
Spearfish	Modern anti-ship and anti-submarine Torpedo in UK submarines
SSAFA	Soldiers Sailors Airmen Forces Association
SSBN	Ship Submersible Ballistic Nuclear – Ballistic Missile Firing Submarine Nuclear propelled
STC	Sea Training Centre of the Royal Naval Reserve
Stingray	An air dropped anti-submarine Torpedo
STUFT	Ship taken up from Trade. A merchant vessel hired for operations by the Royal Navy, e.g. in the Falkland Islands campaign
TAS	Torpedo and Anti Submarine e.g. TAS Officer as a specialization
TCSS	Torpedo Control System, mark number indicates type
TGCU	Torpedo Guidance Control Unit for controlling wire guided torpedoes
Torpedoes	Mk 20, 23, 24 – first generation British anti-submarine weapons Mk 24 known as Tigerfish. Mk 8 – the well tried derivative from World War II torpedoes, an anti-ship weapon. Modern torpedoes are known by a name e.g Spearfish
VC	Victoria Cross
Workup	The period after build or refit where the Ship's Company are fully exercised in Safety and Operational procedures. This is followed by an Inspection to ensure that the ship or submarine is fit to join the Fleet

Index

Page numbers in italic indicate illustrations